Folk Heritage Collections in Crisis

May 2001

Council on Library and Information Resources
Washington, D.C.

ISBN 1-887334-82-3

Published by:

Council on Library and Information Resources
1755 Massachusetts Avenue, NW, Suite 500
Washington, DC 20036

Web site at http://www.clir.org

Additional copies are available for $15 per copy. Orders must be placed online through CLIR's Web site.

The paper in this publication meets the minimum requirements of the American National Standard for Information Sciences—Permanence of Paper for Printed Library Materials ANSI Z39.48-1984.

About the Contributors

Access Keynote Address

Virginia Danielson, director, the Archive of World Music, Harvard University

Virginia Danielson is the Richard F. French Librarian of the Eda Kuhn Loeb Music Library at Harvard University and the curator of the Archive of World Music at Harvard. In these capacities she has overseen the development of a state-of-the-art digital audio studio intended to foster the reformatting of unique recordings. She has had primary responsibility for acquisition, preservation, and cataloging of ethnographic audio and video recordings at Harvard. She has been active in the Association for Recorded Sound Collections, International Association of Sound Archives, Music Library Association, Society for Ethnomusicology, and American Musicological Society. She has participated in university library committees at Harvard that are responsible for preservation and access to nonbook materials.

Ms. Danielson holds a Ph.D. in ethnomusicology from the University of Illinois. Her research has focused on music of the Arab world. She is the author of numerous articles on Arabic song, female singers, and Muslim devotional music. She is a co-editor of the forthcoming volume on music of the Middle East and Central Asia in the Garland Encyclopedia of World Music. Her book *The Voice of Egypt: Umm Kulthum, Arabic Song and Egyptian Society in the 20th Century* was nominated for an Association for Recorded Sound Collections award in 1998.

Preservation Keynote Address

Elizabeth Cohen, president, Cohen Acoustical Inc.

Elizabeth Cohen is the president of Cohen Acoustical, Inc. and publisher of *The Sound Report*, a subscription-only newsletter analyzing the effect of audio on technology and technology on audio-related industries. She is the past president of the Audio Engineering Society and served as the Acoustical Society Science and Engineering fellow to the White House National Economic Council, where her portfolio consisted of arts and humanities applications on the Internet, promoting telecommuting, and accessibility issues. She led the acoustical design teams for Aspen's Joan and Irving Harris Concert Hall and the Academy of Motion Picture Arts and Sciences' Samuel Goldwyn Theater. She is considered one of the premier designers of home theaters. In February 1998 she received the Touchstone Award for her contributions to the music industry.

Intellectual Property Rights Keynote Address

Anthony Seeger, professor, University of California, Los Angeles

Anthony Seeger is a professor in the Department of Ethnomusicology at the University of California, Los Angeles. He received his M.A. and Ph.D. in anthropology from the University of Chicago. His research has concentrated on the music of Amazonian Indians in Brazil, where he lived for nearly 10 years. He was a member of the graduate faculty of the Department of Anthropology at the National Museum in Rio de Janeiro, and became the department chairman and coordinator of the graduate program. He also helped establish an M.A. program in musicology and ethnomusicology at the Brazilian Conservatory of Music.

Upon returning to the United States, he became associate professor of anthropology and director of the Indiana University Archives of Traditional Music. He subsequently served as director of Folkways Records at the Smithsonian Institution and curator of the archival collections of the Smithsonian's Center for Folklife and Cultural Heritage; he is now curator emeritus at the Smithsonian. Mr. Seeger has held executive positions in a number of professional organizations, including the Society for Ethnomusicology and the International Council for Traditional Music. He was elected a fellow of the American Academy of Arts and Sciences in 1993. Mr. Seeger is the author of four books and more than 50 articles on anthropological, ethnomusicological, archival, intellectual property, and Indian rights issues.

Contents

Introduction

Across the nation and over several generations, folklorists, oral historians, ethnomusicologists, and community documenters have been collecting and recording the American cultural legacy on audiotape, videotape, and film and in still photography. Many of these efforts have become the foundation for larger professional, university, and library archives that are repositories for the nation's folk heritage collections. Both the local documentary sound materials and professional archival audio collections are at risk of deterioration and terminal neglect as America enters a new century.

The American Folklore Society and the American Folklife Center at the Library of Congress collaborated on a conference, *Folk Heritage Collections in Crisis*, held on December 1–2, 2000, and gathered experts to formulate recommendations for the preservation and access of America's folk heritage sound collections. They were supported in their work by the Council on Library and Information Resources, National Endowment for the Arts, and National Endowment for the Humanities. This report represents the collected expertise, experience, and wisdom of the participants and proposes a strategy for addressing this crisis in a collaborative way.

The problems that had first moved the American Folklore Society and the American Folklife Center to convene this meeting appeared to relate overwhelmingly to preservation. These were familiar challenges of media degradation and format obsolescence that have eluded effective remediation for at least a generation. To capture living traditions on documentary media, field workers have been using a variety of media formats, none of which is favorable for long-term preservation and each of which has presented new problems of storage, longevity, and hardware dependencies. From the wax recordings of the first part of the twentieth century to the Ampex audio tape favored in the 1970s and the digital audiotape' formats used in the 1980s, these media demand preservation intervention to ensure long-term access. The goal of the conference, it was believed, should be to develop and propagate best practices for preservation to ensure that our national folklore is accessible for future generations.

But preservation, as the experts pointed out, is just one end of the preservation and access continuum. Without a clearer understanding of what kind of access is desired by whom, preservation actions would remain undifferentiated, without priority, and therefore likely without funding. Many collections are poorly documented, making it difficult for researchers to know what materials are available. Librarians and archivists also pointed out that access issues in the field of traditional art and knowledge are complicated by rights issues: the right to use, even the right to record, is not always clearly documented in many of the folk heritage collections most in need of preservation intervention. Too often the various intellectual property rights, moral rights, and privacy concerns of the subject, fieldworker, or repository are difficult to determine or merely ignored for the sake of convenience, yet how can an institution give priority to treating materials without accompanying documentation that would sanction use?

For all these reasons, it became clear that the only way to find effective answers to the problems of preservation would be to look for innovative ways to simultaneously address the contingent issues of access and rights management. *Folk Heritage Collections in Crisis* enlisted experts from all communities that offered to be part of the solution to these complex matters. Archivists, librarians, scholars, recorded-sound technicians, preservation and media specialists, intellectual property lawyers, and recording company executives joined the effort to look at these familiar problems from a new perspective.

To facilitate informed discussion at the conference, the organizers commissioned papers on three major factors affecting the long-term accessibility of folklore collections: preservation, access, and rights management. The papers, reproduced here with the discussions they provoked, were sent to participants before the conference and formed the basis for discussion at three sessions. (The authors were given the opportunity to revise their papers after the conference.) On the second day of the conference, participants crafted recommended actions that are also reported here. As background information for the conference, a survey was conducted of the holdings of the members of several folklore societies and major repositories. A summary of the survey results is provided in Appendix II.

Among the significant achievements of the meeting, perhaps none was as important as the conversation that began among those whose professional interests are aligned but whose professional lives rarely intersect. Bringing together engineers and preservation experts, librarians and archivists, and community folklorists and faculty led to the cross-fertilization of ideas that will be necessary for all those interested in access to heritage materials to move forward. We needed to find new approaches to these old problems, not just call for more money to go at these problems in the same ways as before. Preservation demands tough choices, flexible working methods that allow for rapid integration of new technologies, and scalable approaches. Because fieldworkers and folklorists are themselves constantly making choices about the recording, rights management, and storage of their documentation, they are as intimately involved in these tough choices as are the so-called professionals in archives and libraries. Everyone who has an interest in the long-term accessibility of heritage materials must embrace responsibility for those materials or the recordings will perish.

The meeting occurred within a month after the president of the United States signed the National Recording Preservation Act of 2000, establishing the National Recording Registry at the Library of Congress. This act supports the preservation of historic recordings and directs the librarian of Congress to name sound recordings of aesthetic, historical, or cultural value to the registry; establish an advisory national recording preservation board; create standards for audio preservation; create and implement a national plan to ensure the long-term preservation of and access to the national audio heritage; and establish a national foundation to fund that work. To ensure that folk heritage collections find their proper place in this nationwide effort, the work begun at this conference must continue in an ever-widening series of collaborations across the country, engaging all those whose own heritage is at risk of perishing.

Stating the Obvious: Lessons Learned Attempting Access to Archival Audio Collections

by Virginia Danielson

All of us have experienced compelling, even jolting, intellectual awakenings when confronting primary audio and visual resources that document the lives of people and societies. Art Silverman shared with us the narrative of Marine Corporal Michael Baronowski recounting experience in the Vietnam War recorded on cassette tape in Vietnam in 1966 and sent to the soldier's family in the United States (National Public Radio 2000). Silverman told us of the compelling recording made by William Rathvone recounting his memory of listening to Abraham Lincoln's address at Gettysburg and reciting the speech as Rathvone remembered hearing it (National Public Radio 1999).

An international conference held in Europe brought to my attention another example that has personal meaning. Norwegian Radio preserved the recording of the Nazi officer announcing the takeover of Norway during World War II, assuring citizens that resistance was futile. As an American of Norwegian descent whose great-aunt worked in the resistance, this audio recording gave immediacy and chilling reality to a history that I already knew rather well. Last week, I took a phone call from a former student who had taken a seminar at Harvard in 1978. As part of a research paper, he had made a recording of his Texan grandmother singing cowboy songs. His college-age daughter now wants it for a project. It is at once a part of family history (more valued now than it was when it was originally made by a teenage college student), a record of cowboy songs not widely documented in the literature, and a source of American vernacular music history. More than the straightforward communications and simple entertainments that some of these materials started out as being, the songs and tales, speeches, performances, and events recorded by participants and observers have become treasures of collective memory and heritage. In our universities, faculty, students, and researchers increasingly want to use these materials in teaching to bring home the impact of people and events from the past and in scholarly production as primary sources. Audio and visual materials are both by us and about us in important ways. Families and local communities demand access to materials that they often, with justification, consider their own. Radio stations and museum exhibit curators want to use them. All sorts of people want access to recordings and the materials that accompany them—programs, program notes, field notes, and other documentation—in a convenient way.

Access to these collections, particularly unique archival collections, has rarely been easy. Our fragile audio materials must be reformatted for any kind of use. As John Suter pointed out in his response to this paper, these special collections present difficulties in cataloging and housing and are sometimes regarded by administrators as highly specialized or ephemeral. As such, they have not been given priority for funding or for work. Access usually costs money: for cataloging, for access to online systems, for reformatting. "Most archives," Suter writes, "operate on very small budgets relative to their needs" (Suter 2000:1).

Audio archivists have been plagued by the view that we have no established standards for preservation and therefore should not proceed with projects. This hurts the potential user, who must find out somehow what is in a collection, place a request for the desired items well in advance so that labor-intensive reformatting can take place, then travel to the library during business hours to confront a plain-looking audio cassette and photocopied list of its contents or accompanying materials. Although some institutions will mail copies of materials to users, others cannot. The cassette and photocopies often must be left in or returned to the institution.

Our users' current expectations contrast dramatically with this practice. Many expect fast delivery of MP3 files with scanned images of whatever accompanying documentation there may be. They expect access to contents of collections through free and well-maintained Web sites. Sitting in an institution to listen to materials, not to mention waiting for them to be prepared, never enters their minds as a reasonable option. As a faculty member, researcher, and librarian, I know that, in our hearts, all of us want this immediate access, even those of us who still prefer to read from paper, take notes with pens, and buy books.

To state all of this, especially to a group such as that gathered for this program, is to state the obvious, for all of you live and work with these materials and demands every day. The question is, how do we meet these needs? How do we overcome the multitude of enormous problems that seem to attend every single effort we make at reasonable access? Why is access so hard and what, if anything, can be done to improve it? Of course, myriad technical and legal problems attend online access, which I will leave to my colleagues to discuss. Access to collections and information about them presents its own challenges, some of which I will outline here.

My favorite library patrons will gesture wildly toward a part of our collection and say, "of course, all this will be digitized eventually." As someone working in a large collection, I find this view variously hilarious, pitiable, or depressing. As a nation we have not managed to catalog our collective holdings. We have not managed to complete online conversion of the catalogs that exist. Retrospective conversion and even cataloging are generally less labor intensive than digitizing collections. Our chances for extensive, let alone comprehensive, digitization of primary materials are not good.

A useful starting point for discussion of paths of access may be to acknowledge that everything in our collections does not require the same system of access. Limited access to highly specialized materials may be fine. In-library-only access to sensitive or restricted materials may be the best practice. We probably want to offer wide access to information about the contents of collections through cataloging and inventories. We probably want to offer international, networked access to some parts of our collections. The first step toward establishing what is possible in access to audio collections is recognizing that not everything needs to be treated in exactly the same way. Starting from this point and pursuing, in particular, the issues surrounding networked digital access, what are the principal roadblocks?

To order our thinking, Suter suggests five milestones on "the road toward archival accessibility":

1. creating or acquiring and accessioning important collections
2. processing the collections for complete accessibility in house
3. describing collections online
4. producing detailed finding aids on the Web
5. making archival collections themselves available on the Web

He hastens to add that, although these may appear to be a logical order of work, "in the practical world of an archives, work may be happening on all steps at the same time and sometimes out of order" (Suter 2000:1-2). Suter offers a useful starting point for a discussion of the problems we face.

An immediate issue in any access project for archival collections is that nearly every step of the work requires specialized skill. Simply unpacking and sorting the Laura Boulton Collection of Byzantine and Eastern Orthodox Chant required that we identify which typed notebooks belonged to which recordings, which notes were lecture notes derived from field notes, and then which tapes had been copied from earlier ones and where the other accompanying documents belonged. Ethnic collections often require highly specialized subject and language skills to prepare even the most rudimentary inventory. If the collection is to be cataloged in a standard library catalog, then a skilled cataloger familiar with national utilities such as OCLC and Research Libraries Information Network is needed. Preparing electronic documents requires some command of mark-up language. Preparing and storing digital images requires another set of equipment and skills. Working with digital audio is a bona fide specialization. For networked resources to persist and remain viable, systems of metadata need to be developed and used. A computer programmer is often necessary for using such tools as digital collection management programs. Our sources of inexpensive labor—students, interns, volunteers, and the like—may be but are not predictably suited to this work, especially with large collections that take many months to process.

Labor is always the most expensive component of any initiative, certainly in the long run. Moreover, pleas for more staff members generally require extensive justification and may not be met by budget-conscious administrators who may be under the impression that most work can now be automated and that little human intervention is actually necessary. The expense of audio reformatting is phenomenal. Getting the "last, best play" from a fragile recording may require four hours of skilled labor for one hour of sound.

A common solution to the problem of labor cost is to get a grant. After one has invested weeks or months preparing a compelling argument for a necessarily trendy or attractive part of a collection and assembled the requisite budget, a granting agency may provide the needed help. The problem is that, at the end of the grant, project staff members must depart, taking their skills with them, and the process must begin again in another part of the collection. The maintenance of digital products created by grant-funded projects may itself be a problem.

One might justly argue that some of the necessary skills are quickly becoming common. Many of us can scan a document, burn a CD, and put together a Web site that is fine for rudimentary purposes and may offer decent access to our collections. What if you want your access tools to persist, to be durable and refreshable? One homemade CD probably will not meet this need nor will it offer networked access. Hard links on Web sites eventually lead to nonexistent servers. CD-Rs made just a few years ago may or may not play on every CD player.

Given the cost of labor and the value of our collections, our products must last as long as possible. We cannot afford to make and remake them even if we are able to do so. We need durable audio products. We have seen the failings of cassettes, open-reel tape, CD-Rs, and digital audiotapes. Our cataloging and other electronic documents must be stored in a secure and widely accessible environment, preferably one that can be searched internationally without charge.

There is an important, qualitative difference between building a Web site such as a course page (or even an institutional Web site) and building an electronic resource such as a finding aid. At our university, for example, our finding aid for the Laura Boulton Collection differs from the course page for Professor Thomas Kelly's well-known music course, First Nights. Kelly describes his course page as a pile of rocks, that is, ideas that he and his assistants have tried out, moved around, added, or eliminated (thus changing the shape of the rock pile) in different versions of the site. Mutability is critical to his use of his course site as a dynamic aid to teaching. The Laura Boulton site, on the other hand, is characterized by the goal of near immutability. Unlike teaching tools, library resources need to remain relatively stable over time. We must construct a series of permanent resources. We must finish one and move to another, and so the revising and innovating that is appropriate to the First Nights page would be inefficient for our purposes. We want to select durable technologies and document our choices and procedures well so that the processes of migration, refreshing, and so on can be conducted mechanically if possible. Whereas we welcome the flexibility of electronic formats for adding new data or correcting errors, we do not really want to constantly change our pile of rocks.

Well-organized and accessible housing and storage of physical materials can be expensive; digital storage is a major technological and financial challenge. For the long run, digital objects and metadata about them must be stored securely, preferably in a place where migration and refreshing can be managed automatically. We can learn from radio and national archives in Norway, Switzerland, and Germany that have developed and are using such systems.[1]

Metadata become critically important and we need all sorts of it. We need descriptive metadata: What is it that is stored? We need structural metadata: How do I find this virtual object and what is its virtual format? We need administrative metadata: Who reformatted this object and what equipment was used? Without the metadata, we may as well not bother to create the digital object. Without the metadata, we probably cannot find it, let alone use it or move it.

Cataloging, of course, is a familiar form of metadata in which we record information about the physical and intellectual characteristics of our collections. I suspect that most of our archives produce fairly good catalogs, when there is a staff to do so, and have done so for some time. Our challenges in providing intellectual access are in enabling searches across archives. In the first place, we need databases and library catalogs that present users with familiar formats and familiar mechanisms for finding out what exists. Even though we can now potentially access and use each other's databases if they are online, I have never felt that inventing an idiosyncratic, stand-alone database is a good idea. We need catalogs and databases that are more or less standard, that look or feel similar to each other. The Archives for Traditional Music at Indiana University was the first such collection to enter its cataloging on OCLC. Adjustments of standard library formats—particularly MARC—were necessary, of course, but the result was widespread access to information about the Archives that reached from the university into public libraries and school systems. Nonspecialists could find information about the archives' collection by using a standard library tool. This is surely a good thing. Making use of existing practices, adapting them if necessary, is an effective approach to access. The Association for Recorded Sound Collections (1995) published handy compendia of standard catalog-

---

[1] Communications about these programs have appeared with some frequency in the *IASA Journal* (formerly *The Photographic Bulletin*) and the *Information Bulletin* of the International Association for Sound Archives.

ing rules for audio materials. The International Association of Sound Archives (1999) recently released a more broadly conceived international set of rules that presents a "best practice" without reference to a particular machine-readable format or to practices of a single country or language.

Unfortunately, adapting established practice does not always work. Existing classification systems and such common tools as the Library of Congress Subject Headings, designed as they were for a limited repertory of European arts, fail our highly differentiated multicultural collections. Developing new tools, such as thesauri, is complicated by the different ways in which musicians, folklorists, anthropologists, and local communities think about, name, and classify performances. Creating thesauri on which any part of our community can agree turns out to be very time consuming and becomes work that moves too slowly because few of us can devote the necessary time. Hence, we lack consensus on genre terms and categories for such common concepts as devotional music. What do we do about Arab-American Muslim communities that refer to their Sufi rituals as *dhikr* whereas their Turkish-American co-religionists call the same phenomenon *zikr*? In the Indian communities, we find Sanskrit-derived names that are also written in Tamil script and have English versions. Systematic transliterations of the Sanskrit and Tamil names produce two different Romanizations, and the English version may be different still. We can decide to use Anglo-American Cataloguing Rules (AACR2) to establish the name; however, who is going to verify that the multiple variants represent the same person? Representing our various local communities accurately is hard and searching is harder.

Electronic finding aids constructed to the standards of encoded archival descriptors (EAD) are a good alternative. EAD offers a looser, more narrative, and adaptable format for inventorying collections than does standard cataloging. However, producing the proper diacritical marks for the names and terms of a Vietnamese or Hmong community in EAD finding aids is nearly impossible at present. Does this matter to us? Designations from the Human Relations Area Files have been useful for organizing access to ethnic collections; however, these are old and sometimes incomplete. The terms can be too puristic to suit multicultural communities. As archivists, we may easily feel stuck, that everything we do has something wrong with it. We make very little progress in our collections without running into an insurmountable wall that seems to preclude access to a collection.

Partly in response to such issues, Suter draws attention to the need for our access tools to feature blunt pointers to general groups of records likely to include what the researcher is seeking. "A too-sharp pointer, one that takes a researcher to the precise item she or he is seeking, is very expensive and difficult to create, and more important, it means the researcher doesn't need to look through all the other interesting materials in neighboring boxes or folders" (Suter 2000: 5). As an inveterate browser of index screens in online catalogs, I find Suter's point compelling.

Attempting to step out of the morass myself, I would like to describe an initiative that our library launched in 1999. Called "Music from the Archives," it attempts preservation of and access to some of our unique collections. I offer this not as a prescription but as an experience and as a set of decisions that might start our discussion. Music from the Archives engages digital technology to offer a model for access. It was not conceived as a comprehensive program through which everything we have will be digitized; rather, it tries to advance ways to offer wide access, intellectually and virtually, to selected items from our collections. Our selections proceed from the strengths of our collection, which in turn proceed from the priorities of our primary constituency: the faculty and students of the Harvard music department and the related larger research community.

The contents of a collection will be presented in an electronic document that follows the format of the electronic finding aid. It draws on national standards and practices for the creation of EAD documents and serves them from Harvard's Online Archival Search Information System (OASIS), which includes Harvard's other finding aids for archival collections across the university. Audio files of selected performances and image files of field notes and other documentation will be available through links from the finding aid. Ultimately, we want to create a thoroughly integrated multimedia finding aid—one that may use the technology emerging in the Making of America projects sponsored by the Digital Library Federation—in which the digital resource itself will be conceived as having multiple manifestations. Whereas now we can move from one set of digital objects to another, our plan is to produce a more flexible tool that will allow us to show relationships among parts of our collection that may not be readily apparent to the user—for example, among a festival program book, a photograph, a concert program, and a recording. We will thus be able to bring parts of our collections to the attention of users quickly and graphically. Digital standards and systems for metadata for our images have been developed in consultation with the Harvard University Library Digital Imaging Group. At the music library, we did not try to develop or invent these procedures. We did, however, develop our own audio preservation studio because we considered ourselves and our colleagues to be more reliable resources than any existing at Harvard. Our studio is centered around a Sonic Solutions high-density audio workstation that allows us to sample at 88.2 kHz and to digitize audio at 24 bits, which enables us to capture sound at a high rate in superb detail. The engineer typically reformats recordings onto two CDs (for users) and two computer data tapes (for storage). This form of tape is much more robust than any other we have. Real Audio streaming sound files are produced for networked use. Metadata are captured about all processing performed on the file so that it will be possible to recreate the labor-intensive decisions made by the audio engineer.

One result of our project will be the production of research-intensive tools. Our documents will have several important features: They will offer entire musical sources rather than short samples. Researchers will actually be able to conduct research, not simply browse collections or sample holdings. Although not every item from every collection will be networked, every item will be inventoried and we will be able to add audio files on request.

Another result is that our digital products will be durable. With very modest investment of time and money, we can make two copies of the CD using products from two different manufacturers and two copies of the exabyte tape using two different lots of tape. Although no particular claims for longevity can be made for CD-Rs or computer data tape (let alone Real Audio files), we feel some confidence that one of the four exemplars we produce will persist until a viable remote, robotic repository is available. Certainly these formats are most convenient and accessible, and possibly hardier, than the open-reel tape of our originals.

We seek solutions to the problems of digitizing, storing, refreshing, reformatting, and migrating digital objects over the years. Beyond creating access to resources, we seek to regularize the processes of work that are necessary to create the digital products, using our existing permanent staff wherever possible. Creating a new flow of work and bringing together regular library staff members in the production are goals as important as the resources themselves. For these productions we do not want to rely on temporary project staff members whose skill and training departs with them when the project is over; a permanent staff can contribute to this new kind of work over the long run. To summarize our goals, we seek to use digital technology to develop a new model of access to rare audio collections, produce useful electronic resources, and institutionalize the process of work that emerges. Durability is an important result. To achieve it, attention to the choice of digital audio formats is critical. Once formats are chosen, a durable system of identifying, characterizing, and locating them—that is, systems of metadata—must be constructed that will function for as long as we can manage. I have sought ways to develop this project for the better part of 10 years. Only recent circumstances and priorities in my institution have rendered it finally possible. Our work is inextricably linked to the time and place and the character of the institution in which we work. What is possible one place does not work in another, and our project at Harvard may not make sense in other contexts. What broad ideas from Music from the Archives might help us move beyond local constraints?

To make effective progress with our collections, it may help to make selections based on our collections and constituencies. Each of us working selectively from strength may produce a good corporate result for access to our collections. Storage of archival collections often predicates access, and labor (to alter storage systems by reformatting) is expensive. These two factors suggest that access and preservation or storage decisions and actions should be made simultaneously if possible.

We should work together and rely on each other, as no one institution is likely to have all the necessary expertise or facilities to provide all of its own paths to access. For the short term, creating multiple digital formats may answer our needs for access and persistence if we are careful about the equipment and processes that we use. Most physical formats have become inexpensive to use. For long-term digital access we need storage facilities. Might we work collectively to persuade public and private agencies to build digital repositories that we could all use?

To make long-term use of such facilities, we need to master systems of metadata. For these expensive enterprises, we need to have an ideal in mind from which we retreat as necessary when costs are prohibitive or processes inappropriate to the desired long-term result. The simplest, cheapest alternative may be the one we have to take. (Even well-endowed institutions have budget constraints.) However, simplest and cheapest is not a fertile place to begin a thoughtful planning process. We need to consider the possible best alternatives in concert with what we can do immediately and practically to lead our institutions forward effectively.

Certainly, we need to retool ourselves a bit for these tasks. We also need to find ways to acquire or share the services of specialists such as audio engineers, computer programmers, and subject specialists. We as individuals cannot become all of these people. We need to bring specialists into our environments by hiring them or, more practically, by establishing regional centers of service and consultation to which the smallest archive might have affordable access. We need to fashion workable collaborations that produce results rather than years of committee meetings that yield nothing we can actually use.

REFERENCES

Association for Recorded Sound Collections. 1995. *Rules for Archival Cataloging of Sound Recordings*, 2nd ed. Annapolis: Association for Recorded Sound Collections.

International Association of Sound and Audiovisual Archives. 1996. *Information Bulletin*. Baden Baden: International Association of Sound and Audiovisual Archives.

______. 1999. *The IASA Cataloguing Rules: A Manual for the Description of Sound Recordings and Related Audiovisual Media*. Compiled and edited by the IASA Editorial Group convened by Mary Miliano. Stockholm: International Association of Sound and Audiovisual Archives.

National Public Radio. 1999. Gettysburg Eyewitness. Produced by Jay Allison. Available from http://www.npr.org/programs/Infsound.

———. 2000. The Vietnam Tapes of Lance Corporal Michael A. Baronowski. Produced by Christina Egloff and Jay Allison. Available from http://www.npr.org/programs/Infsound.

Suter, John. 2000. Response to Virginia Danielson's "Stating the Obvious: Lessons Learned Attempting Access to Archival Audio Collections." Presentation at the conference *Folk Heritage Collections in Crisis*, Library of Congress, Washington, D.C., December 1–2, 2000.

ACCESS:
Summary, Responses, and Discussion

Summary

Virginia Danielson began the summary of her paper with the acknowledgment that as she wrote the paper, she thought of entitling it "Failing Laura Boulton." Part of the Laura Boulton Collection is housed at the Archive of World Music at Harvard University, and the Archive's first major digitization project was designed to get a significant portion of this collection online. As is common with digitization projects, there was a steep learning curve. Many of the lessons about access that she imparts in her paper were learned the hard way and, to some extent, at the expense of Laura Boulton and her heritage. The Archive digitized everything in the collection, and the process took three full-time employees 18 months to complete. When she assessed the progress made and the price paid, Ms. Danielson had to conclude that, despite their best efforts, they had failed Laura Boulton by not providing effective access. By May 2001 that will be rectified: a multimedia finding aid will be mounted to enable ready access to the collection.

Ms. Danielson underscored the key themes of her paper:

- Preservation must begin now because we cannot afford to wait until a better technology comes along.
- Digital access must be selective for ethical, legal, technical, and financial reasons; comprehensiveness should not be a goal.
- Digital storage costs may go down but labor costs will not; we must strive for cost-effective approaches to digital access.
- Identifying technical skills needed—from programmers and engineers to cataloging staff—must come early in project planning; outsourcing will be inevitable.
- Digital access is an added value and fees for service should be considered to offset the costs.

She advocated for libraries to be clear about what is necessary to do as opposed to what is only desirable. The former should not be sacrificed for the latter. She called for common archival repositories for digital storage available to all types of collecting institutions and communities.

She made several additional observations that need to be addressed in considering how to widen access to folk heritage collections. Among the technical concerns that both folklorists and librarians mention is that although EAD (encoded archival descriptors) may be a fine thing for collections of text-based materials, it does not work for folklore. The field needs to develop a new document-type definition for sound recordings. Another community concern is that the field has not developed a controlled vocabulary that permits ready subject access. This must be attended to quickly. As cataloging departments are downsized in libraries and networked search and retrieval protocols gain ascendance, catalogers become "content people," subject experts who are essential intellectual peers. Ms. Danielson urged her colleagues to become involved in developing and using descriptions of collections that are acceptable to the communities they represent and are also readily understandable by users.

Responses

Art Silverman, National Public Radio
John Suter, New York State Archives

Art Silverman, the senior producer of "Lost & Found Sound," spoke of the access needs of users—from radio producers like himself to the many listeners and researchers who depend on the work of Ms. Danielson and her colleagues across the country. After admitting that he risked stating the obvious, he discussed lessons he and his colleagues have been learning while seeking access to archival audio collections for his radio show on our aural environment and its past. Dependent as radio producers are on private and public collectors, they are even more dependent on deadlines and their ability to find suitable materials under pressure. The promise of digital technology to capture faithfully and preserve without distortion over time is almost magical, as is its promise to enable the quick retrieval and easy sharing of sound files.

Speaking from the point of view of a consumer, he urged an expansive view of what to collect and preserve. There is no way to know what will be important in the future, and the opportunity for regret is enormous. At the same time he cautioned that preservation must also be selective, because rich archives that are inaccessible—not cataloged, searchable, or readily retrievable—might as well not exist. So, how do we find a happy medium?

"Lost & Found Sound" can serve as an example. In a sense, the call by the producers for listeners to submit their precious audio collections created a collection. The producers empowered millions of individuals to act as curators of their own folk collections. When National Public Radio accessioned the materials, they suddenly faced the same difficulties as other collecting groups. They have a bewildering variety of media, from wax cylinders to 78-rpm recordings to Dictaphone belts. They came to see that the art of good collecting is knowing what to discard. Trying to create natural triage and intellectually sound ways to narrow the choices in audio is hard because we have been dealing with audio for only a few generations. There is as yet no audio trail comparable with a paper trail. Hence the promise of digital storage that Ms. Danielson touts may put off for decades the painful choices of what to preserve.

In the meantime, it will be important to save some examples of the original analog artifacts of sound, such as cylinders, discs, and 8-track tapes—artifacts that might be called the audio equivalent of first editions—together with original playback equipment that can recreate the original acoustic experience. The voices we hear from the 1890s are distorted because of the frailties of analog equipment; it will be important to consider what our present-day digital fidelity will mean to sound in the future. Radio producers can help raise current awareness about the importance of our audio heritage and so raise support for funding the work involved in collecting and preserving.

Mr. Silverman claimed that the most useful tool he could imagine now would be a simple online reference guide to audio collections. This guide would be a one-stop catalog for collections and would use an understandable controlled vocabulary, or common language, that would open up the world of sound to all.

John Suter, former director of the New York Folklore Society and now of the New York State Heritage Documentation Project, focused his remarks on what the professional librarians, archivists, and folklorists could do to make concrete advances in access to folk heritage collections. The underlying theme of his remarks was that access is about audience and sustainability. The general health of folk heritage collections is jeopardized by their low status within academia, reflected in the fact that the academic departments, such as ethnomusicology, that rely on these collections are often relegated, literally, to the basements of music departments. As borne out by the survey conducted for the conference, funding for collections and staff is also at or near the ground-floor level.

Mr. Suter proposed five milestones of accessibility for collections:

1. creating or acquiring and accessioning important collections into archives
2. processing the collections for complete accessibility in-house
3. describing collections online with collection-level records in MARC or other standard formats
4. mounting detailed finding aids on the Web
5. making archival collections themselves available on the Web

All institutions, regardless of size and wealth, face the fundamental challenges of identifying collections, bringing them into the archives, putting them into some sort of intellectual and physical order, and making finding aids. Perhaps only well-funded organizations can get to stages 4 and 5, but they will find stages 1, 2, and 3 every bit as difficult as will their smaller peers. Mr. Suter underscored how important it is in the fields of folklore and ethnomusicology that solutions to technical problems, such as cataloging and description, be scalable to small as well as large collecting institutions. Citing the evidence gathered in the survey before the conference (see Appendix II), he pointed out that the folk heritage collections that are in crisis reside in myriad small institutions. These collections can reach the milestones of accessibility only if all members of the communities represented at the conference actively pursue collaboration and open communication.

Turning to steps essential to achieving accessibility, Mr. Suter called for a thorough grounding of folklorists in the basics of archival practice and terminology. He pointed to the work done in New York State and available in print, *Working with Folk Materials in New York State* (Suter 1994) and *Folklore in Archives: A Guide to Describing Folklore and Folklife Materials* (Corsaro and Taussig-Lux 1998), as good starting points for folklorists. It is important to develop and sustain partnerships with professional archivists. He advocated publicizing the value of folklore materials not only to folklorists and ethnomusicologists but also to historians, linguists, genealogists, musicians, and crafts people, among others. Increased demand for these materials will inevitably lead to more resources being devoted to making them accessible. Such access cannot be provided without developing a thesaurus or controlled language in which to describe the materials. He echoed Ms. Danielson's call to use terminology that is transparent—a blunt pointer, he said—because the universe of folk materials is very large and sparsely populated. A thesaurus must make items used by ethnic groups with different traditions of transliteration readily accessible to nonspecialists. The thesaurus project, while widely supported in the professional community, has run into some resistance by those who wish to make the vocabulary refined and perfectible. Mr. Suter urged that we not let such concerns keep us from beginning the hard work of creating the thesaurus.

Speaking of the promise of digital technology to make folk heritage collections more accessible and thus build awareness of them, Mr. Suter recommended that institutions that could afford to put collections online strike a balance between attempting to do whole collections—which, as Ms. Danielson pointed out, can slow the effort and be extremely resource intensive—and doing what is in effect an anthology. Making selected and annotated collections accessible can make intrinsically valuable materials readily available to a new audience while being an effective marketing tool for the entire collection, the repository, and folklore in general. The opportunity to inform casual Web users about the provenance of the materials and the effort behind the images and sounds, from documenting and collecting to preserving and describing, should always be a focus of such Web publications. The ultimate goal of increased access is to make the stuff of folklore a universally valued part of our common cultural heritage. Ultimately, that is the only way to secure its preservation and accessibility.

Discussion

The issues of greatest moment to the participants were those of identifying what collections exist, creating efficient means for accessing them, creating a thesaurus, and using the Web for access.

Identification, Selection, and Inventories

Participants were sobered by how small a portion of the folklore universe was captured in the survey conducted—all of it unpublished—and how inaccessible even those collections appear to be. Some called for doing a general inventory of collections that would include published materials, especially all the ethnic materials recorded before the Second World War. Given the instability of the commercial market, how frequently companies were bought and sold, and how spotty the record is about what happened to the inventory, this seems a daunting task, although private collectors, many of whom are well-known, may have a lot of information about commercial recordings. The Association for Recorded Sound Collections has agreed to seek funds for compiling a national discography of 78s.

Another aspect of that problem concerns selection: scholars, and, to some extent, collectors have their fashions and changing interests and may not even collect some of the materials that will turn out to be of special value. Are we about to lose the history of white jazz because we accord black jazz greater status these days? Compiling information about whatever it is that is held in public and private hands as well as information about what was commercially recorded, whether or not it exists in a collection, is essential to defining the parameters of ethnic music.

Bibliographical versus Sound Access

Some participants argued for making collections accessible by putting them online and providing direct access through sound whereas others argued that this is a self-defeating and financially unrealistic approach. A fundamental cleft exists between those who wanted to solve the problem of access by dumping things online and those who hold that bibliographic access, while not exciting, is still the only way to build a sustainable network of access for all. Both camps agree, however, that there is a need for greater commitment of institutional resources to mounting sound collections online to build awareness, constituencies, and so forth. Perhaps if regional collections would federate to mount holdings online, they could achieve economies of scale and solve the preservation as well as the access issue by pooling resources. The online environment, while very enticing, is fraught with many uncertainties. Certainly, the ongoing legislative battle over Napster and other file-swapping technologies challenges the notion that increased online access will lead to increased funding. On the contrary, some participants pointed out, the public will continue to assume that music, spoken word, and other audio should be available for free.

Descriptive Practices

Those who argued for a concerted effort to increase bibliographic access pointed out that EAD needs considerable refinement to make it work at the item level for audio recordings and that there are promising new forms of description that may be more flexible for sound. Among those mentioned were the Dublin Core, guidelines published by the Association for Recorded Sound Collections, and international rules proposed by the International Association of Sound Archives. It was noted that there is a need to harmonize or merge descriptive practices with standards used by the Society of Motion Picture and Television Engineers and Audio Engineering Society, and with other metadata standards.

Thesaurus

Agreement was widespread that creating a thesaurus is a critical first step in widening access to folk heritage, and participants moved to lower barriers to working on this important tool. There was consensus that an ethnographic thesaurus would be a terminology list for folklorists and ethnomusicologists that would be flexible to allow deviations for local adaptation. It would allow nonspecialists to access finding aids and collection descriptions. Although some debate occurred about how expansive or narrow and how technical or secular the terminology should be, all participants recognized that other disciplines had faced similar challenges of scope when creating their controlled vocabularies and that this group needed to consult with groups experienced in other fields.

Portal

One of the most promising ways to solve several problems facing folklorists would be to create a portal. This would enable one-stop shopping—also described as the Yellow Pages for folklore—for information about collections and would provide a place for small institutions that cannot create a significant Web presence to find a place in the larger universe of collections and expertise. The portal would include information about what repositories hold and would provide guidelines for collectors and donors about how to document and prepare their collections, sample release forms for subjects, and so forth.

On several occasions one participant expressed the need for some tool to be created or information to be gathered and another participant said that such a tool already existed or some publication had appeared with just that information. One example was a call for information about the key elements of audio folklore documentation; the American Folklife Center published such information in *Folklife and Fieldwork* (Bartis 1990). The portal would allow for free flow of expert information among specialists in different areas. Knowledge transfer between scholars and preservationists, folklorists, and archivists appears to be a chronic problem and a major barrier to moving ahead with solutions. The portal would bridge this gap and also provide knowledge transfer to small and midsized organizations that cannot afford specialized staff.

Problems always have to be solved in bringing such an idea as a portal to life—who will do the work, where the portal will be located, where funding for long-term maintenance will come from. These problems are solvable.

Scalability

Because the scope of folklore is so great (one participant pointed out that it should include industrial as well as so-called community lore), the only way to deal with access issues is to break the problem down into regional collection and description responsibilities. It will be easier to build support for access among those who have the closest connections with the materials, and we need to empower local communities to grapple with access and not abandon attempts because they fall outside the purview of various professional folklore networks. This again argues for scalable solutions to access issues.

REFERENCES

Bartis, Peter. 1990. *Folklife & Fieldwork: A Layman's Introduction to Field Techniques.* Washington, D.C.: Library of Congress.

Corsaro, James, and Karen Taussig-Lux. 1998. *Folklore in Archives: A Guide to Describing Folklore and Folklife Materials.* Ithaca, N.Y.: New York Folklore Society.

Suter, John, ed. 1994. *Working with Folk Materials in New York State: A Manual for Folklorists and Archives.* Ithaca, N.Y.: New York Folklore Society.

Preservation of Audio

by Elizabeth Cohen

The goal of this paper is to focus attention on the practicalities of preserving recorded folk collections. In that spirit, I throw down the gauntlet: the key to preservation is distribution. Moreover, the challenges of preserving recorded folk collections are not primarily technological; they are found in the analog domain and they are mostly aesthetic. The search for the perfect technical solution is a diversion from the painstaking work and art of transfer. If anything, budgetary and acoustopolitical issues hamper our progress in doing what must be done: migrating the collections into the digital domain. A corollary to this is to migrate the collections into the digital domain with uncompromised fidelity.[1]

Let me digress with an anecdote. A few months back, I spoke with a curator who was deeply concerned about the problems that continue to paralyze us in preserving audio information: the need to preserve materials in their original format; the obsolescence of playback machinery; the risk, in the digital realm, of being unable to define a faithful copy. The discussion took the form of the litany, "Computers are unreliable, the risk of loss is too great, mediums change too quickly, the costs are too high, we can't even play back our recordings (digital audio tapes, VHS, beta, 8-tracks…) from two years

---

[1] Uncompromised fidelity offers several advantages. Innovations in signal processing are heading toward full 3-D image restoration. We should not discard information that may be essential to future sound field reconstruction. The future may offer a way to restore the environment and hence more of the emotional nuances of a recording. Using greater bit depth and higher sampling rates is advantageous. For example, an engineer can raise the level of recorded material without losing resolution, which prevents audible noise from becoming part of a recording. More bits improve the performance of signal processing algorithms by providing more information to work with. This is important for accurate restoration and avoidance of distortion-induced artifacts. There are more intelligent ways to achieve cost savings than compromising on the fidelity of an archival master.

ago. We need our temperature- and humidity-controlled storage for original tapes, media with 100–200 year life expectancy, invincible encryption, unlitigatable no-thrash copyright access." Feeling mischievous, I asked, "What controls the thermostats in your intelligent, climate-controlled conservation room?" My question was met with silence, and I had to suggest that in all likelihood it was a microprocessor: one of those pesky computers was leading the chain of command and was fundamentally responsible for preservation. To be practical, we must recognize that there is no escaping the role and rule of computer technology in the preservation of recorded folk collections. The first hurdle is to recognize the absolute integration of the computer and the computer network into twenty-first century life.

Although it may fall to some of us to deal with the "what ifs" of an electromagnetic pulse tragedy, our collections are far more likely to survive the scars of mayhem if they are robust and alive in many hands. Moreover, to delay the transfer of analog media into the digital domain until it has reached perfection and reliability is to compromise preservation. The more time that passes, the more we allow the further degradation of analog materials.

Distribution is the key to preserving audio folklore collections in the twenty-first century. In fact, distribution is preservation. Moreover, this is the type of preservation that keeps the art alive and not sterilized in a glass case in a passive museum setting. Fortunately, in the networked world, distribution is becoming both easier and cheaper. Our technical concern has shifted to studying the best methods of providing efficient access. Do we want multiple server nodes where folklife information is stored or a single location for a master server farm? Will libraries become storage service provider utilities or will they lease space on new electric company-like utilities?

In the networked world, information can be maintained and distributed electronically; it no longer needs to be centrally located. Archives may no longer need to secure information in vaults. Collections may be located in a thousand places. Digitization forces a paradigm change. Librarians are used to thinking that copies are not the real things. The cult of the original is powerful in the world of analog recording, where information was lost with each generation. Today, however, the original digital material may be preserved in its pristine form anywhere and everywhere.

The good news is that it does not take a rocket scientist to make the choices outlined above; the bad news is that we must still contend with the warped strands of technophobia and politics. I find it painful to listen to the liberal archivists' search for the Holy Grail medium that will never decay and for which they will never have to maintain machines. I find it more painful to listen to the conservatives launch into another paean to analog tape as the only medium we can trust. These polar beliefs are evidence of an unwillingness to face the task of conversion into the digital domain.

There is no choice but to accept that data migration is the only intelligent policy. We know how to do this to exquisitely fine resolution; banks do it every day. Computer companies upgrade with every significant revision of code, and when the hard disk is full—or when cheaper and faster storage capacity is available—they do one thing: copy and transfer their data. Likewise, consumers adapt to technological change. In the twentieth century, 78-rpm records gave way to long-playing records, then CDs, then DVDs; music can now be accessed from streaming and downloading MP3s. The lifespan of consumer physical digital media is estimated to be 5 years or less (Library of Congress 2000). We do not know what the recording medium of choice will be in 10 years, not to mention 20, but we do know that it will facilitate the transmission of, access to, and storage of bits. Therefore, it is necessary to adopt a device-independent policy for the migration of digital audio data based on robust error correction capability.[2] The archival modality must have enough depth to render uncompromised audio quality. Today, for this stage of migration, we are assuming capture at 24-bit 192 kilosamples.[3]

Folklorists must remain vigilant and acquire the budgets for flawless transfers. All the original information must be retained. There is no scientific reason for loss of quality; only sloppiness or value engineering can intervene. Economies of scale can be achieved in a few basic steps:

- Identify and set priorities for the items to be preserved.
- Clearly define your technical criteria for the archival master.
- Recognize that you are in the preservation business and identify your market.
- Negotiate for group rates with rerecording facilities. This includes recording studios, postproduction facilities, and independent consultants. Negotiate with the various sound unions to establish reasonable rates for small archives and libraries.
- Demonstrate the size of your industry. Unless there is an accurate inventory, engineers will not invest in the personnel and infrastructure to go into the preservation business. Students will pursue other areas of sound engineering because there is no assurance or awareness of a viable field of endeavor.

All digital audio materials should be preserved through migration before the decay of the built-in error correction. As long as one operates within the error correction envelope, the original material can be restored, copied, and preserved indefinitely with no loss of information. Error correction also makes it feasible to detect degradation before information loss occurs. Standard algorithms and flagging devices that detect and correct information loss already exist.

With this knowledge, it is possible to establish a policy for data migration of digital audio materials. This policy will enable curators

---

2 Error correction is a well-developed technology that enables detection of signal degradation and enables the user to act before vital information is lost.

3 Some people may think that 192 kilosamples is overkill, but a cohort of researchers and musicians believe that inaudible harmonics may affect brain function. Although I do not think the research is very credible, I believe we should be better safe than sorry. Four times oversampling is a spit in the ocean of bandwidth.

to plan for the data migration necessary in the age of digital audio. It will also prevent the growing intractability of our audio archiving problems.

Why We Cannot Afford to Dawdle

One hundred years of sound recording has left us with a legacy of the equivalent of more than 5 petabytes of professionally recorded audio. Libraries are already overwhelmed with preserving everything from cylinders to vinyl. They are drowning in a preservation crisis as they continue to accumulate media in extinct formats and as audio materials proliferate at a pace they are unable to match.

There is no mercy; according to J. A. Moorer of Sonic Solutions, it is estimated that we are distributing terabytes (TB) of new garage band music each day (personal communication, September 28, 2000). Three million new Web pages appear daily, and a growing percentage include streaming audio (Lyons 2000:146). Currently, 4,271 radio stations "broadcast" their signal on the Internet, up from 2,615 stations a year ago and up from a mere 56 in 1996 (BRS Media Inc. 2000). In autumn 2000, Arbitron's Web site reported that 25 percent of the American population (57 million) had listened to Internet audio; 20 percent (45 million) listened to radio stations online and 13 percent (30 million) listened to Internet-only audio.[4] Information appliance companies are initiating music delivery to phones, to personal digital assistants, and into an array of portable entertainment devices.[5] Lest you think that 64-kilobit audio is the sole character generator that is stimulating the data storage industry, the surround sound community is creating its own information-rich recordings. With the standard sample rate shifting to 192/96 kHz, 24 bit, and 4.76 GB of audiovisual data per DVD, multichannel audio is swelling the data banks as well. As FedEx Chief Information Officer Robert Carter said, "There is this tidal wave of storage demand coming at us"(Lyons 2000:146).

In the mid-1990s I wrote about the likely appearance of unlimited and ubiquitous bandwidth in my arguments against adopting nontransparent compressed audio for new systems such as high-definition television. In October 2000, EMC Corporation Senior Vice President James Rothnie was quoted in *Forbes* as saying that by 2005, the world's bandwidth could grow a millionfold, making it "virtually free and virtually infinite." Storage, he believes, will follow suit. He estimates that the total capacity sold annually could grow 50-fold in five years, from 200 to 10,000 petabytes—enough to hold the text of 500,000 Libraries of Congress (Lyons 2000:153).

---

4 Statistics are frequently updated on Arbitron's Web site: http://www.arbitron.com/webcast_ratings/home.htm.

5 Audio is a key component in the avalanche of new wireless hand-held devices being offered to satisfy consumer demand for mobile broadband music and information. See to-be-published proceedings of "Audio for Information Appliances—Challenges, Solutions, and Opportunities," March 2001, the Audio Engineering Society, http://www.aes.org/events/18/.

Storage Media Choices for Customer Use, Interim Storage, and Preservation

Data storage is getting both cheaper and more space efficient. Disk density has nearly doubled every 15 months for the past five years while the cost per megabyte fell 52 percent every year during the same period (Goldman 2000). Today's 3.5-inch drives are almost 600 times denser than the 14-inch mainframe drives of the 1980s. IBM's Ultrastar 72ZX holds 73 GB, enough room for every original Frank Sinatra song ever recorded or all of Steven Spielberg's movies on DVD (Goldman 2000). We are rapidly approaching storage capacity of 1 terabit, or 125 GB per square inch.

The cost per megabyte of storage capacity has decreased from about $30 in 1987 to $0.005 today. Even more remarkable is the decrease in the size of disk drives. In the summer of 2000, IBM released a 1-GB Microdrive for $499. The Microdrive has the dimensions of a matchbook and weighs less than 1 ounce. According to IBM and as reported by Daniel Lyons (2000) in *Forbes*, its spinning platter, the size of a quarter, can hold the equivalent of 18 CDs. IBM aims to double the storage capacity of the Microdrive every 12 to 18 months. To date, manufacturers of digital cameras, personal digital assistants, and two MP3 players have adopted it.

Current Practice: Tape

Magnetic tape seems to be the interim, if not archival, system currently used for digital storage. Business systems include Exabyte Mammoth-2, Quantum DLT (digital linear tape) 8000, Linear Tape Open, and Sony AIT-2. Tape technology is derived from two branches: helical tape and linear tape. The former is heir to higher density and performance whereas the latter pledges greater reliability.

Many studios are using Exabyte tape drives for a wide range of audio archiving purposes including backup, data transfer, and preservation tasks (Exabyte 1996–2000). I have been told that Abbey Road has more than 2,500 Exabyte tapes. Individual musicians are using both the 8-mm Exabyte tape and the Mammoth M2 225-m tape cartridge formats. For dealing with interim exigencies, Exabyte tape offers advantages: Mammoth-2, for example, uses a two-level Reed-Solomon error correction code. Exabyte's error correction code corrects errors on the fly by rewriting the blocks within the same track. Data-grade tape, such as AME, stores more data per cartridge. Its anticorrosive properties improve tape durability and reduce tape wear, allowing the media to achieve a 30-year archival rating. Depending on the Exabyte system, reliability ranges between 250,000 and 500,000 hours. This is measured in mean time between failures—the greater the number of hours, the more reliable the drive.

Universal Mastering Studio's Paul West is currently using Sonic Solutions archiving software on Exabyte tape and then transferring the content to his mainframe system and onto a Digital Dynamics Processor. However useful Exabyte is as a transfer medium, some users shudder when thinking of it as an archival medium. One user commented, "It seems you can sneeze and lose a file." From a librarian's point of view, it is a device that is available only from one company that is extremely vulnerable to the vicissitudes of the stock market. On the other hand, if distribution is preservation, then it is a transfer medium with a potential 30-year lifespan.

Sony Music, under the leadership of David Smith and Malcolm Davidson, has begun transferring Sony Music's assets into its digital audio archives using an automated tape library system. The archival system consists of a Sun Enterprise 450 server connected by SCSI to SONY DTF tape drives integrated into an ADIC AMI/E automated media server. The design of Sony's ADIC Automated Media Library is based on the goal of infinite file life, which allows "systematic monitoring and timely replacement of media, with secondary copies, or complete transfer to new technologies"(ADIC 1999). Sony is able to automatically evaluate the quality of the backup tape before it deteriorates. Each cartridge is evaluated regularly by looking at the raw error rates. If the raw error rates grow over time, an exact copy of the tape can be made and the old tape can be deleted. With 600 TB of data on 200,000 cartridges, there was no choice but to automate the error correction (ADIC 1999).

Current Practice: Magneto-optical Disks

Magneto-optical disks may play a role in systems of audio preservation and distribution. They are less expensive than hard disk drives and can provide between 20 and 40 years of viable storage. In the future, blue laser magneto-optical disks will quadruple the amounts of storage capacity.[6]

The Audio Engineering Society (2000) released its *Standard for audio preservation and restoration—Method for estimating life expectancy of magneto-optical (M-O) disks*, which is based on effects of temperature and humidity. To develop this standard, a sampling of 80 disks was baseline tested for byte error rate. The standard gives a graph that can be used to estimate the time for a given percentage of disks to fail.

Data Storage Technology: Optical Media

Optical disk material includes CDs, the entire DVD family (DVD, DVD-R, DVD-RW, etc.), and the previously mentioned magneto-optical drives. Use of optical media is extremely convenient and getting more economical every day (DVDs were selling for $.15 to $.19 at the beginning of 2001). However, only 20 years after the commercial birth of the CD are we getting standards about its life expectancy. Pretty absurd!

Standards regarding DVDs are at the initial stage of the drafting process. The good news is that with a little common sense and use of manufacturers' recommendations, we have a very useful medium

---

6 Because blue lasers have shorter wavelengths, it is possible to focus on smaller spots and therefore store more information on optical media.

for preservation by dissemination.[7] If we agree on eternal preservation of contents, then the projected 50-year lifespan of optical media is certainly user friendly (Murray 1994). In addition, manufacturers are listening to the concerns of musicians and music librarians and are offering professional-quality, archival-life disks such as the Kodak Ultima.

However, the lifetime stability of optical disks is not dependent merely on the disk itself. As is clearly covered in the introduction to the draft international standard ISO/DIS 18925.2 Optical Disc Media Storage, it is system and user dependent. Frequent handling, piling, and heat affect CDs and DVDs. In addition to human behavior, the system components include the disk material, equipment on which the disk is run, software, and storage environment. Life expectancy for optical media also depends on light, corrosive gases, and particles.

The National Imagery and Mapping Agency's National Technology Alliance recently issued a CD entitled *Data Storage Technology Assessment 2000* (Sadashige 2000). Included on the CD are assessments of storage media environmental durability and stability; current state and near-term projections for hardware technology; and a review of magnetic tape, hard disk drives, optical media, optical write-once disks, solid state and emerging technologies, and future possibilities for data storage. "Efforts by the recorder and media manufacturers in the area of data capacity per unit volume improvements are directly transferable to the library (mass media storage system) capability improvements . . . by the year 2005, the floor space requirements for a one petabyte capacity library system may be as small as ten square feet" (Sadashige 2000:5).

Preservation Strategies

The development of successful preservation strategies will require the cooperation of computer scientists, data storage experts, data distribution experts, fieldworkers, librarians, and folklorists. Technology needs to be transferred from the information storage and transportation businesses into the folklife domain. Banking, security, and critical services industries all have dealt with the issue of preserving vital information. We must draw on their experience in developing policies of backup and redundancy and in addressing human interface issues.

The Research and Development Agenda

We need to work with research and development efforts across a variety of disciplines. For example, exciting work is being done in haptic simulation, which someday will allow us to virtually touch and work with virtual objects. We will be able to receive tactile feedback in playing virtual machines or musical instruments.

---

[7] Dissemination is a method of preservation clearly different from preserving an archival master.

In conclusion, we have examples from other industries on how to archive. There are no technical barriers to archiving. The technical aspects of this problem have been solved. Capitalism is providing cheaper, faster, and more reliable modes of storing, accessing, and distributing audio. A social decision must be made to migrate materials into the digital domain or it will undoubtedly be done without the aesthetic guidance of the folklife community. The genie is already out of the bottle. If you want a voice, it is time to do the work, not just talk. It is time to approach preservation as a business.

REFERENCES

ADIC, Inc. 1999. *Preserving Musical History: Digital Asset Management for Intellectual Property at Sony Music, Inc.* Available from http://www.adic.com/US/English/Collaterals/Case_Studies/Sony_Music.pdf.

Audio Engineering Society. 2000. *Standard for audio preservation and restoration—Method for estimating life expectancy of magneto-optical (M-O) disks.* Available from http://www.aes.org/standards/reports/AES-STANDARDS-IN-PRINT.html.

BRS Media, Inc. 2000. *BRS Media's Web-Radio Report Strongest Growth Segment of Webcasting Is Radio.* Press release, San Francisco, September 29. Available from http://www.brsmedia.com/press000920.html.

Exabyte. 1996-2000. *Data Storage Basics.* Available from http://www.exabyte.com/products/overview/index.cfm.

Goldman, Lea. 2000. Driving Hard, Driving Fast. *Forbes* (Oct. 2):152.

Library of Congress. 2000. *Planning Culpeper's Digital Archives: The National Audio-visual Conservation Center. An Overview of Digital Planning and the Digital Prototyping Project.* http://lcweb.loc.gov/rr/mopic/avprot/culpplan/culpweb/sld009.htm.

Lyons, Daniel. 2000. BOOM. *Forbes* (Oct. 2):146-53.

Murray, W. P. 1994. *Accelerated Service Life Predictions of Compact Discs.* ASTM STP 1202:263-76. Philadelphia: American Society for Testing and Materials.

Sadashige, Koichi. 2000. *Data Storage Technology Assessment 2000.* National Technology Alliance, National Imagery and Mapping Agency. Available from http://palimpsest.stanford.edu/byform/mailinglists/av/2001/01/msg00000.html.

PRESERVATION:
Summary, Responses, and Discussion

Summary

Elizabeth Cohen began the session on preservation by forcefully asserting that the time to worry about analog transfer is over. While recognizing the importance of analog formats for those who hold historical collections, she nonetheless felt that technophobia was contributing to the delay in transferring masses of analog information to digital format for present day and future access. There is no reason to fear that it will be impossible to preserve digital audio. She urged the audience to look to businesses, many of whose chief assets are purely digital, such as banks and record companies. These businesses migrate their data regularly and they incur no irreparable losses.

The chief barrier to preserving audio collections is not technology, as sound archivists repeatedly tell her. It is the reluctance of these archivists and preservation experts to move forward with the technology, even as it changes. Serious funding constraints exist, of course, but she believes that resources can be mustered when and if the message gets across that these materials are endangered and we cannot afford to lose them. She urged those dedicated to preserving sound to recognize that anything left on analog media will soon be orphaned.

Ms. Cohen made several suggestions for lowering barriers to moving to digital format. She recognized that changing operations to digital is very expensive and that the best sound equipment, the kind that industry more or less takes for granted, is out of reach for most of the institutions represented here. Reaching out to industry to forge partnerships would be the way to approach some of the hardware and software challenges. If the folk heritage communities could aggregate their demand for preservation, then industry would find the quantity of work an inducement to partnership. Going to industry individually will not work, but heritage institutions should not assume that industry would not welcome a concerted approach. Ms. Cohen also recommended that the community make an aggressive case for the importance of these materials. Those who have helped create folk heritage collections and who use and preserve them are best positioned to advocate for the preservation and distribution of these collections.

Finally, she noted that the distribution of sound will continue to get easier with the growth in bandwidth. She predicted that within three years MP3 will be an obsolete format, compression will be a thing of the past, and costs of converting to digital format and migrating data into the future will drop significantly.

Responses

Mark Roosa, Library of Congress

Mark Roosa took up Ms. Cohen's notion of preservation as distribution by recalling the experience of libraries in the past few decades with brittle books. A coordinated, nonredundant effort to preserve embrittled books on microfilm has led to a greater efficiency in capturing the information. Adhering to community standards of filming and storage and making copies readily accessible to other libraries served both preservation and access. Mr. Roosa noted that before standards for filming and storage had been developed, much microfilm had been created that was substandard, and libraries are facing the consequences of that every day. Although distribution or proliferation may encourage survival of our recorded folk heritage, without coordinated distribution and a willingness and commitment among creators and institutional stakeholders to share in the maintenance of digital files, preservation will not be automatically ensured.

Mr. Roosa expanded on how the relationship between preservation and access is changing in the digital realm. Preservation often means supporting preservation needs for access rather than stabilizing the intrinsic value of an item. In the digital environment, originals often lose their intrinsic value by evolving into a version that best serves the end user needs, not that most closely identified with the occurrences of a historical event and that best conveys the essence of that event. This has serious implications for preservation, and the call to proceed with digitization risks ignoring the implications. Will that become a source for future regret, the way that nonstandard microfilm is today?

Although the "cult of the original" is still operative in libraries and among their patrons and may be a damper on moving ahead into the digital future, powerful practical forces also are slowing the pace of change. Mr. Roosa said that the Library of Congress staff is planning to move audio and visual resources into digital formats for preservation. However, it will take them 50 years to extract all the information they have in analog formats and put it into digital form. Going fast is not an option. Moreover, the library, as large as it is, cannot make the transition to the digital realm alone. The management of digital files, be they surrogates of originally analog sound or digitally generated, should be integrated into one system. That system must be integrated into the network of systems outside the library that will include both the creators and the users of the materials. Again, the development and common adoption of standards are prerequisites to building such systems.

Most formats developed today meet the needs for access but are not suitable for preservation, at least as we currently understand the term. Even though the costs of data capture and storage are dropping in the commercial sector, it is hard to gauge the effect of these trends on preservation in libraries and archives. Data simply do not exist yet. The costs of training staff, selecting and preparing historical materials for transfer, and creating metadata are high and are unlikely to decrease because they depend on human skills. The unrelenting changes in technology that are driven by market forces cause preservation experts anxiety in light of the uncertain fate of these formats in 50 and 100 years. The preservation community cannot be daunted nor can it wait for stability. Mr. Roosa argued for preservationists to engage the digital challenges and bring to these issues the same principles of reversibility, suitability of application, and respect for original intent that inform their work in the analog realm.

Discussion

The general discussion revealed a consensus that digital format is, indeed, the future of audio preservation, but there was considerable dissension about when this will happen, how it will happen, and who will be in control of the technology—commerce alone or commerce meeting the needs of preservation. Some preservation experts expressed the view that the solutions Ms. Cohen said already exist in the commercial market are in fact access solutions and not preservation solutions. They do not want to see the consumer market setting standards to which they must conform. Others question whether preservation versus access is not a false distinction in the digital realm. The two cultures—technology and heritage—seem once again at odds. All participants agree, however, that reconciliation between the two is imperative, and confronting their differences in a constructive dialogue is the first step toward working together. Many of the groups holding the most valuable and endangered materials are presently not equipped to provide proper physical storage let alone digital storage.

One archivist from Europe agreed that migration is the only possible solution for sound archiving and that within the domain of European broadcasting, this has worked well and the archivists have had great input into how this is effected. In Germany there has been successful self-checking and self-regenerating in mass digital storage since 1992. Another archivist asserted that preservation of historical material in digital form is just as dependent on developing appropriate metadata as it is on bit integrity, which means involving subject experts as well as technicians.

Participants agreed on three fundamental issues that completely transcend the technical issues of how. They are selection (what to save), how to document and preserve the source materials, and how to pay for all this.

Certain formats are more vulnerable than others and must be given priority for reformatting. These include cassette tape (completely unpredictable), instantaneous discs (such as lacquer), cylinders, and acetate tapes. It was proposed that an urgency matrix be developed and posted on a Web site. This matrix would match preservation needs to an estimate of required outlays (that is, time and money) so that budgets could be projected into the foreseeable future and treatments could be given priorities. The engineers expressed the view that the first step is for archivists and folklorists to do a needs assessment of collections and share that information with technicians.

An effort must be made to bring together the needs of large and small archives so that they can be addressed cost-effectively. Is there an emerging business in data archiving and storage that can serve the preservation community's needs? Although there is talk in the library world of developing common digital repositories for text-based electronic publications, no comparable talk is occurring among sound archivists. On the other hand, the Library of Congress has received private and public funding to build an audiovisual preservation facility, known as the Culpeper Facility because of its location in Virginia, that is conducting work that can be scaled down to other organizations. That work includes specifying how to prepare analog and digital materials, transfer them onto new formats, capture metadata, assemble an archivable digital object to deliver quickly, manage a digital repository, and negotiate access from both technical and legal points of view. Information about this work is regularly reported on the library's Web site. Once the community can vet the standards that the library proposes for its internal operations, the standards can be adopted or modified as best practice and used when looking for vendors.

Although the Library of Congress may be able to offer fee-for-service preservation in the future, building regional service centers will still be necessary. Partnerships with industry may help defray costs, and partnership with those who most value the materials can also lower financial barriers. Enlisting religious organizations, for example, that can find volunteers to inventory unprocessed items in need of preservation can speed the process of getting started.

Another area of great concern is how expertise in legacy technologies is transferred to a younger generation. People from many disparate domains should be able to use professional meetings and publications to share expertise about technical and selection matters.

Intellectual Property and Audiovisual Archives and Collections

by Anthony Seeger

Introduction

We are in the midst of an intellectual property gold rush. Thousands of fortune seekers are trying to stake their claims to promising territory, existing claims holders are seeking increasingly aggressive means of defending their claims, and the original owners are often being ignored. Scholars and enthusiasts whose work uses intellectual property and archives and libraries that store it are largely bystanders in this gold rush, but they are profoundly affected by it.

Most archives, in particular, find themselves in the position of a horse being kicked forward and reined in at the same time. When you kick a horse and pull back on its reins, the horse gets confused and may rear, buck, rear, kick, and forget all its previous training. Faced with the tremendous challenges of preserving disintegrating collections, prodded by increasingly entrepreneurial administrations to be more self-supporting, kicked by patrons for not having more online, and reined in by concerns about copyright and ethical uses of their materials, archivists rarely buck, but we do roll our eyes in frustration, consider other jobs, and may forget what we have learned through decades of work with our collections, with depositors, with patrons, and with communities.

This paper is about intellectual property and audiovisual archives[1] and collections.[2] It will not resolve your preservation and ac-

---

[1] Throughout this paper, audiovisual archives include institution-based archives with collections of audio recordings, video recordings, photographs, paper records, and other materials related to systematic collections that often combine several media. Audio, visual, and photographic media all share certain features in the area of intellectual property as well as in preservation and access; the paper records here are not given as much emphasis.

[2] A collection is any kind of private collection that has not yet been deposited in a specialized institution such as an archive. This could be the researcher's field tapes, the jazz collector's 78-rpm record collection, or any other systematic collection.

cess problems but I hope it will clarify them. It will not advocate any particular technological direction, because technology is changing quickly enough to make such recommendations dated between my writing them and their publication. It will advocate that archives take proactive stances regarding intellectual property but, especially in the area of training, review their own contracts and other archive forms and carefully evaluate proposals for use of materials they hold in trust for communities, scholars, and collectors. It will advocate that archives help researchers obtain the rights they need when they do their research and transfer those rights required by the archives at the time of deposit in a way that permits maximum access. It will also recommend that archives help artists and communities learn what their rights are and how to protect them. It will advocate that researchers and other collectors review their collections now and take steps to resolve ambiguous rights questions. It will advocate that our academic programs focus on intellectual property as part of the study of music, folklore, anthropology, and other fields. It will also argue that archives should look at the new technologies and the new pressures placed on archives in the light of their accumulated knowledge, collections, and expanding potential to affect the lives of their users.

There is no question that the changes in the U.S. copyright laws, pressures to adopt emerging international copyright agreements, and pressure to extend the protection of copyright to more and more material for longer and longer periods have already had a significant effect on archival operations. The Internet's potential to disseminate information rapidly and widely raises intellectual property issues with an urgency they have not had before. The situation is further complicated by the age of the collections in most audiovisual archives (older rather than newer, with greater significance given to old material than to new) and by the only slowly changing practices of field researchers and those who collect materials and deposit them in the archives.

The issues surrounding intellectual property and audiovisual archives cannot be divorced from the specific features and objects of archives and collections. These issues are too important to be left to lawyers alone because they are not only legal (what people can do) but also are ethical (what people should do). The interests of the large companies involved in the intellectual property gold rush are also rarely the concern of the patrons of and contributors to archives, whose opinions must be championed.

Two Kinds of Collection—Two Kinds of Challenges

Before going into my subject in any more depth, I want to make a distinction between two different types of collections, because the issues raised by each type are quite different. To a certain degree this distinction classifies types of archives and also clearly distinguishes some archives from libraries.

Commercial Recordings and Other Publications

Some collections consist largely of commercially released recordings and associated print and photographic materials. Such collections may be created from the compulsory deposit of published materials (for example, at the Library of Congress), by the accumulation of commercial recordings for broadcast (for example, at commercial radio stations), or by collectors who devote themselves to systematically amassing recordings of a given genre or period. These collections have an important feature in common—the print and recent audio publications are governed by laws of copyright. The laws are reasonably clear, albeit inadequate for the digital age and our patrons, whether we like them or not. Collections of this sort can be treated similarly to how large libraries handle print materials.

Some problems arise, though, even with commercial recordings. Before 1972 no national copyright law governed actual sounds on commercial recordings, although the compositions were covered by existing legislation. The compositions, cover art, liner notes, and song sequence were all covered by copyright but not the sounds themselves. Local antipiracy laws covered the actual sounds. Also, different countries have different laws regarding the use of older recordings—thus it is possible to reissue older sound recordings in Australia or Germany that cannot be reissued in the United States.

Most archives, like most libraries, follow copyright laws carefully, because they are part of larger institutions with little reason to embark on long battles with the well-funded legal departments of large corporations. This can be frustrating for patrons, who find that such policies limit their access to and use of materials. Among the frustrations of patrons are the relatively small amount of a piece that is considered to be an idea covered by copyright; the difficulty of identifying the copyright holder of material published by a company that has ceased to exist under its original name; and the lack of response from many copyright owners, who often do not even answer requests for permission to use materials they control unless a lot of money is involved. Countless researchers have told me about their inability to get an answer from the major record labels when they ask to use the materials in limited educational editions or from publishing companies for the use of musical transcriptions and song lyrics in books and journals. It is also difficult to ascertain which compositions are in the public domain and thus available for free use. Sometimes several music publishers claim the same composition, which occasionally turns out to be in the public domain by virtue of an early publication. To further complicate things, the arena for fair use is being constricted by the holders of the copyrights whenever possible. A solution similar to that of the Copyright Clearance Center, which has greatly facilitated the creation of course readers by handling clearances for many academic publications, would be a good model for easing these frustrations. However, no centralized effort has yet been undertaken to permit quick and easy use of copyrighted audiovisual materials.[3]

---

[3] The success of MP3 and Napster may encourage such a change.

Individual collectors of published recordings often respond more flexibly to requests for use of these materials than do archives. Under a liberal interpretation of fair use, collectors can copy their recordings, which they then send to researchers who need the copy to analyze—something most archives will not do. Collectors often cite this liberty as a reason not to place their collections in an archive. A potential drawback is that an individual is not an institution, and the best collections should eventually end up in institutions that will care for them over long periods.[4]

Unpublished Collections of Recordings, Manuscripts, Field Notes, and Photographs

Quite distinct from collections of published materials are collections of unpublished and unique materials. Such collections include the scholar's field recordings of interviews, performances, and events; the enthusiast's collections of concert tapes; and the scientist's recordings of experiments. The Archive of Folk Culture has acquired many such collections as have the Indiana Archives of Traditional Music and, to a lesser extent, archives at the University of California, Los Angeles; the University of Washington; the University of Illinois; Harvard University; and elsewhere. Local community scholars, museums, individuals, and institutes of various kinds may also hold such collections.

Because the recordings have never been published, the type of use permitted for them is often unclear. Possession of the recordings does not permit collectors or archivists to use them however they wish. The following paragraphs describe some of the rights that need to be transmitted from the artist (the individual or group recorded for whatever purpose) and collector (the person responsible for making the recording and depositing it in an archive) to the archives:

Artist: To transfer rights, the artist must possess the rights to the performance, which may not always be the case. A performer might record material belonging to another group and thus not have the rights to transfer to the collector. The artist recorded must be able to transfer to the collector the rights the collector requires for documentation.[5]

Collector: The collector needs to have the artist agree to not only make the recording but also to transfer to the collector the rights that are needed. This usually means for personal research use but should also include deposit in an archive for preservation and future consultation. It would be wise to include publication in print or other media. If the conditions are not agreed to, either in print or on the re-

---

4 Collectors should deposit their materials in an archive while they are alive. It is much easier to accession a large, systematic collection when the depositor can help with its organization and interpretation.

5 This might include permission from the material's creator if the artist is recording someone else's work, but the complexities of research are such that the researcher really has to determine, with the artist, what needs to be done to ensure that the materials can be used.

cording itself, it is often difficult to get them later. The collector should also find out whether the person being recorded is able, within the local knowledge system, to give the rights granted with the recording. The collector should note reservations—such as "people can listen to this song, but it can't be used for profit, because our church doesn't allow that" or "you can't publish this without coming back to me for permission." These restrictions should be noted when the recording is made and when it is transferred to any institution or individual.

Archives: Archives usually receive materials from collectors rather than artists. An archive needs to ensure that it can make copies for preservation and that it can provide access to the collection, preferably in the broadest sense, using technologies both existing and as yet to be invented. If possible, archives would like to be able to permit the commercial use of the recordings in collaboration with the collector and artist. Without the explicit transfer of these rights, including a statement that the depositor is authorized to grant these rights, the archive will find itself frustrated in its efforts to make its collections accessible. Archives need well-designed, easy-to-understand contracts that give them the rights they need and give the collector space to provide the information on restrictions and reservations that may have been expressed during the recording.

There are real ethical issues here. If the artist puts restrictions on something, the collector or depositor and the archive should take every step possible to respect those wishes. This may be seen as an impediment to dissemination, but it should be a fundamental tenet of archival policy.[6]

Contracts should be drawn up with the interests of all parties in mind. When I was director of the Indiana University Archives of Traditional Music, I was frustrated by the number of collections that had been deposited with the highest degree of restriction on the whole collection. This was often because the researchers who made them wanted to publish their results before others could use their collections. They would restrict the collection and then forget to change the restrictions after they had published their results. As part of a broad effort to improve access, I contacted every depositor we could find to renegotiate the contract. The objective was to permit increased access to at least part of every collection while allowing continued restrictions on material that needed to continue to be restricted. I also created a new contract that required the highest level of restriction to be reevaluated every 10 years. I did not anticipate the Internet and after my years at Folkways would probably rewrite the contract again, but I was able to improve access to the collections by retroactive contract negotiating.

---

6 Such restrictions may also be viewed as violating rules of public accessibility. However, in putting relative weights on access and following the wishes of the artist, I always put the artist's intentions first—they are primary requirements for establishing trust and maintaining working relationships with scholars and communities. This is also the position taken by the code of ethics of the American Folklore Society.

The Enduring Cultural Bias of Copyright Legislation and Its Implications for Archival Recordings

The following discussion of copyright is meant to show how the existing laws came from a culturally defined idea of creativity that is not shared by most folklorists, anthropologists, and other scholars. The thinking behind the laws comes from an earlier time; was influenced by a romantic ideology; and has been reinforced by evolutionist thinking, which presumed that earlier forms of social life were inferior and would inevitably change. The social philosophy of the past centuries, long abandoned in other areas, is still expressed in international legislation. Scholars and archivists alike need to recognize that they cannot simply abide by current legislation but need to work to bring the legislation into the twenty-first century within a postcolonial global economic system in more than merely technological ways.

Any discussion of copyright law must be placed in the context of the societies in which the currently observed laws were developed. They should be seen as the production of a specific group of people in specific societies at a particular moment in their histories. Ideas about intellectual property were developed and codified in Europe and the United States and have become the framework for international intellectual property law.

Today's copyright laws reveal their origins in the Enlightenment, when philosophers looked to the individual rather than the group as the fundamental element of society. They were further developed in England and France during a period of tremendous social and political change. The laws took much of their current form in a period of increasing urbanization, literacy, and evolutionist thinking. The laws addressed only new creations by literate creators that were printed on paper and sold commercially to a literate public. The initial purpose of copyright was to allow the printers' guilds time to recover their investment before others could make copies of the materials. The early copyrights established the trend for copyright in the ensuing centuries: publishing companies held the protected copyright, which usually applied to print publications. After a fixed period, copyright material would enter the public domain and become available to anyone for making copies or using in other forms. This is an important part of copyright and patent law: the restrictions are temporary to enable the creator to benefit from the creation and after a fixed time the restrictions expire so that the public may benefit from the free flow of information.

Any folklorist or anthropologist will immediately notice that quite a lot of human knowledge and wisdom was not included in formulations of the copyright law including the creations of the illiterate and nonliterate, ideas created and controlled by a group rather than individuals, and protection of knowledge not intended for commercial use. Not only were these left unprotected, they were specifically made available for creative artists to use without restriction to produce new materials that could be copyrighted. Let me give some specific examples:

- The laws either failed to consider or specifically excluded all of what is broadly called folklore and traditional knowledge. The laws controlled the right to make copies of written original material, not the right to retell stories heard around the campfire or in the local pub or the right to learn a song from a songwriter in a local oral tradition. This kind of knowledge, often labeled collective knowledge or considered traditional, was placed in the public domain where creators of new works could freely use it.

- Laws carefully protected the rights of individual, literate composers in the name of that composer (or the composer's publishing company). However, laws did not recognize the possibility that a lineage, clan, village, church, or some other social group (other than corporations, which were recognized) might possess knowledge that should be protected in the name of the group.[7]

- A composer can make some changes in an unpublished traditional song and copyright the only slightly altered song without any consideration of the original performers of the song. In so doing, the composer is able to ignore the identity of the original owner (if identifiable) or any claims the original community might wish to claim to the song. For example, a composer might take a sacred song from a South American Indian community and turn it into a commercial for replacing the rain forest with cattle pastures. This can be done without acknowledging either the original creators of the work or the possibility of any objection on their part that their own sacred art forms are being used to destroy the land they hold sacred. It may be legal under current laws, but is it right?

In sum, intellectual property legislation encouraged and continues to encourage the creation of new things and creates a disincentive to value traditional performances—because the creations of traditional artists are not valued. Value is often concrete: a popular music songwriter can make money from a song; a traditional artist who performs an equally moving song cannot receive any songwriter's royalties. The traditional artist often learns from a teacher who has learned from another teacher. Copyright law should protect both their performance and the knowledge they have obtained because their artistry does not lie in new creations. Without such protection they do not benefit from the exploitation of their art, and tradition must be abandoned in favor of innovation in order to protect their art.

Over the centuries, music publishing companies have extended the life of their copyright protection (originally only a few years, now 70 years) to reduce the amount of material in the public domain and restrict fair use of intellectual property to control it. The most

---

7 The very idea of collective authorship, or lack of individual author for orally transmitted works, may well have been an inheritance from evolutionist thinking, which often worked through oppositions. Civilized societies acted one way and thus primitive societies must be based on the opposite principles. This was assumed to be the case in social organization, thought processes, and many other spheres. Thus if nineteenth-century authors created individually, it was assumed that evolutionarily less-developed societies could only repeat or create collectively rather than individually.

recent revision of the U.S. copyright laws included an extension for company control and few concessions to the rights of artists or communities, particularly those that are nonliterate or traditional.[8]

There is a colonial aspect to the copyright laws. Colonizing countries used the colonies to provide raw materials for their industries and in turn sold their finished products to the colonies at a profit. Colonies were often prohibited from developing their own manufacturing capabilities in the interest of keeping them dependent. In music a creator can take unprotected, public domain materials and create something new from them that can be protected. Anyone who wishes to use the adapted original materials must pay the person who adapted the material, not the original creator or the original creator's heirs. The issues have become particularly acute in the area of pharmaceuticals. Here, the knowledge of traditional curers is considered public domain. Once that knowledge has been taken and turned into a product, the traditional knowledge bearer receives nothing, and the pharmaceutical company may make millions over the discovery, which was in fact something learned from a member of another community. Here again, laws developed by countries with large pharmaceutical industries (who have strong lobbies and can afford political contributions) affect the lives and futures of small communities in countries that are threatened with reprisals should they even consider changing the legal status quo. The serious ethical issues regarding pharmaceuticals are being played out around the world. Similar things have happened in music when a popular performer takes folklore materials from books and recordings and creates a popular arrangement.

Are There Other Formulations of Intellectual Property?

Many societies have extremely elaborate concepts of ownership and control of knowledge, many of which bear little resemblance to the European and North American ideas of copyright. Among the more elaborate are those found in Melanesia. For example, on Vanuatu, payments must be made to original producers or their community for such things as the use of a particular design in wood carving or the wearing of a certain flower. The archive of the Vanuatu cultural center has a tabu room where restricted recordings are placed to demonstrate their secret and restricted nature (Amman 2000). Australian Aboriginal communities often restrict knowledge of certain materials to a certain group of people (a clan, a phratry, a gender). To the rest of them the information is secret. Such restrictions are also common in American Indian communities. Such examples are fur-

---

8 American copyright law continued to be dominated by print publishing companies until well into the twentieth century. Hymnbooks and later the huge success of sheet music brought them wealth and influence. The major 1909 revision of the U.S. copyright law did not specifically legislate about recorded sound but it did protect music publishers. They may not have seen the significance of the wax cylinders and discs, but by the end of the twentieth century, recording companies owned most of the large music publishers.

ther evidence of how culture shapes systems by the definition and control of intellectual property.

Throughout the world today, traditional musicians, the subjects of interviews, and the subjects of photographs and films increasingly feel that they are being deprived of income through an unjust copyright system. They see how those whose rights are protected can become very wealthy whereas those whose rights are not protected appear to remain poor. They find it increasingly difficult to find successors who will carry on their arts, partly because no one can make a living at it. One reason they cannot make a living is that their art is not recognized by, protected by, and paid for through copyright law and the equitable distribution of royalty payments.

Some countries, especially former colonies of Europe, are making an effort at the national level to protect local traditional performances. This has usually involved the creation of a paid public domain arrangement in which no music may be used for free: if there is no named composer, then the payments must be made to the nation. So far, however, these funds have not been distributed to traditional communities or artists in any systematic way. These countries are also leading an international movement to fundamentally change the existing copyright laws to include what is now deemed to be traditional, unprotected knowledge. Both the UNESCO and the World Intellectual Property Organization have been investigating and preparing recommendations for the protection of what is variously called folklore, intangible cultural heritage, and several other terms. Their work is far from complete and may result in other difficulties, some of which are identified in a very thoughtful paper by Michael Brown (1988), such as a reification of authenticity, and conflict regarding hybrid forms.

What Does the History and Current Status of Copyright Law Have to Do with Archives?

Quite a lot. Imagine[9] that the maker of an X-rated film wants to use a recording of a traditional religious song in a sex scene in a bordello. The best performance of this song is found in your archive or collection. The producer offers you $20,000 for the use of the recording in the film and the accompanying sound track (an enhanced CD with explicit photographs to browse while listening to the music). What should you do? Should you make a digital copy and use the $20,000 to fund badly needed preservation? Should you refuse to do so and confirm patrons' views of archives as places where material is placed never to be available to anyone again? What would you do if the film were a documentary history of bordellos, no money was offered, but the music was desired to portray life in a bordello next to a church on Sunday morning? Would that be any different? (Hint: You certainly should not start by contemplating national copyright codes.)

---

[9] One can imagine any number of scenarios—some of them political, others cultural. Most have nothing to do with sex or theology, but this one will do as well as any other to highlight the issues.

The place to start, of course, is with the original recording and deposit agreements you should have in your files. What did the collector and church community agree to at the time of recording? What did the collector require the archives to do when the recordings were deposited? Many of the holdings in research-based archives are on the one hand unprotected public domain materials and on the other hand to some degree governed by local ideas of ownership and propriety. The archives' rights to use the materials are often further affected by restrictions placed on the use of the materials by the collector or donor of the materials.[10] This places the archive in a position of arbiter between the traditional ideas of ownership, restrictions of the donor, and current copyright law.

For these reasons, archives have to be especially careful to consider the rights of the original performers as well as the rights conferred by law before entering into any agreement. It might be perfectly legal for a film company to play a traditional religious song in a scene filmed in a bordello, but would it be ethical to use the one you have? Would it respect the original intent of the recording and the reason for its deposit in an archive?

It is precisely the ambiguity of the archives' holdings that should place them at the forefront of the debate about the ethics as well as the legal implications of the copyright code. I am particularly happy to find the Library of Congress the locus of this discussion of copyright laws.

Who Is Our Audience? Why Are Our Collections Important?

What archivists know and few others seem to realize is that archives can be places of discovery, excitement, and joy. The public image of archives is all too often of a dark place where one sends things that are no longer needed. When I was directing the Indiana University Archives of Traditional Music, I was impressed by the number of musicians who came to listen and learn from the collections, by the request from the Fox Indians for copies of some cylinders so they could perform forgotten songs, by African archives' requests for copies from our collections to enable African countries to possess the documents of their own musical heritage.

The history of many communities has been transmitted through oral traditions rather than written documents, and audiovisual archives provide access to the speech, music, and visual images that communities can use to understand the past and fashion the future. Social scientists have long recognized that communities engaged in changing themselves often look to the past as a model through

---

10 For example, at the Archives of Traditional Music, many collections were deposited with use restrictions on the entire collection. In cases where public domain material whose use would be permitted by the local community was protected by a deposit agreement restricting access or where permission is granted only to listen to the recordings but not to transcribe any of them or obtain a copy for analysis, the archives cannot permit any other use.

which to create a coherent future.[11] In this light, archives become a resource for the recovery of history and the establishment or reestablishment of a degree of cultural autonomy. At Indiana University I felt that we were supplying communities around the world with the tools for their self-determination. Using documents of their own history, they might be able to forge major transformations or establish meaningful continuities.

As a scholar I have been humbled by the significance of some of the by-products of the research of anthropologists and folklorists. One hundred years after their publication, few articles in the *Journal of American Folklore* or the *American Anthropologist* are of more than minor interest. The recordings made by some of those authors, however, often continue to be very exciting to scholars, musicians, and members of the communities in which they were recorded. Over time, it may be the collections we have made rather than what we have done with them for which we are most gratefully remembered. This requires many of us to rethink our priorities and pay attention to the fate of our recordings, photographs, and unpublished materials.

In reacting to the various pressures on our institutions and personal collections, it is essential for archives and collectors to remember the future audiences for these collections and their potential effect. It is well to recall the trust in which we are holding them. Our ethical treatment of the artists and the communities from which they have come must be of primary importance in our positions on intellectual property, decisions about preservation, and strategies for institutional survival.[12]

Archives, Multimedia, and the Internet

Clearly, the emerging and rapidly evolving technologies of multimedia and the Internet offer archives the chance to maintain the unity of their collections and yet make them available on a scale previously unimagined. It allows us to facilitate access not only to information about our holdings (through online catalogs) but also to many of the materials themselves. The technology, however, is far ahead of the archives' ability to use it. Our collections are rarely ready for the kind of wide access that is potentially available. One of the ways in which they are not ready is that we usually do not have the right to distribute them that way.

---

[11] An early example is Karl Marx. In the opening paragraphs of *The Eighteenth Brummaire of Louis Bonapart* he writes "just when [people] seem engaged in revolutionizing themselves and things, in creating something entirely new, precisely in such epochs of revolutionary crisis they anxiously conjure up the spirits of the past to their service" (Marx 1972 [1851]: 437). Although he criticizes this tendency, he is right to note that it often happens.

[12] A dean at Indiana University once told me that it was not very interesting to know that people all over the world used and respected the Archives of Traditional Music. Why, he asked, would the people of Indiana want to serve the rest of the world through an archive? As always, I realized, thinking has to be global but action has to be local. Within a year I had acquired a large collection of Hoagy Carmichael manuscripts, papers, recordings, and memorabilia (Hoagy Carmichael was a native son of Indiana and a beloved university alumnus) and the world-famous Archives of Traditional Music was on a much sounder institutional footing in the university, the State of Indiana, and, by extension, the world.

We can look to technical solutions, but many technical solutions—like audio streaming to avoid copying—are surpassed by technologies that defeat them more quickly than we can adopt them. It is also possible that a technologically superior system will not become the standard, because the consumer market continues to influence the media received by most archives and the recordings made by most collectors. Despite this, archives need to continue to experiment with new ways of reaching the people who will use and benefit from their collections. I recommend nonexclusive contracts, however, and experiments with the parts of the collection for which rights are quite clear.

As we experiment with different systems for digital distribution, we can be reviewing our contracts; acquiring collections with more clearly established dissemination rights; and working to bring the needs of our peculiar institutions to the attention of lawyers and lawmakers, scholars and the people they record, and communities and their members. The next section makes a number of specific suggestions; readers are welcome to contact me with more suggestions.

Steps to Be Taken by Archives, Collectors, and Institutions to Facilitate Our Use of New Media

Archives alone will not resolve the general issues of intellectual property nor will they even resolve their immediate problems with acquisitions and dissemination. Access to research-related collections will have to be ensured through a broad collective action and changes in the public's attitudes toward information. It is difficult to predict how this will play out in the coming years. One thing is highly probable, however: there will be an enduring need to clearly establish what rights are being transferred to collectors and archives. Given this probability and the problems faced by archives and collectors today, here are a few suggestions for archives, collectors, and professional organizations.

1. Archives should bring the issues of access, preservation, and dissemination to the attention of colleagues in the disciplines they serve. They should argue for ethical as well as legal and practical approaches to the materials in their possession. The archiving committees of the Society for Ethnomusicology and the American Folklore Society are good forums for discussing these issues as are specialized professional organizations such as International Association of Sound and Audiovisual Archives. Archives and collectors should be involved in local discussions regarding intellectual property and should contribute their own expertise to such discussions. Archives should provide rights information and rights transfer forms to researchers before they start their work and should pay careful attention to ethical issues when materials are deposited. Archives should also mobilize to help artists and members of communities that are being recorded understand how to protect their rights; at the same time, archives should educate

members of communities about the uses of archives and show how properly written agreements can both protect the community members and permit the archive to do its work.

2. Archives should be very cautious in signing agreements for the use of their materials. Most such agreements require the archive or collector to affirm that it controls the desired rights, and most archives do not have a paper trail to prove that should the issue become contested. Archives might want to consider reviewing their collections and creating new contracts for collections they would like to make widely available through digital archival distribution. Archives might consider collaborating in creating standard licensing agreements for archival material, with the assistance of legal counsel, that protect their interests as well as those whose materials they hold. Archives might want to review their acquisitions policies. If they have a regular supplier of materials (such as recordings of university concerts, for example), they might want to ensure that all the appropriate rights have been transferred to the archives for the desired use.

3. Archives should take advantage of technological developments that support their goals within the limits of sound policy and ethical practice. Technological solutions to intellectual property issues have had a short life, however, and will probably not resolve access concerns by themselves. Collection samples, in the form of 30-second audiovisual segments and low-resolution photographs, appear to be commonly accepted, although this may change.

4. Archives will certainly face some censure by insisting on following both ethical and legal guidelines. Archives should take the lead in deflecting criticism by consulting the ethics guidelines of the American Folklore Society, Society for Ethnomusicology, and American Anthropological Association and by using brochures and Internet sites to explain the reasons for their policies on intellectual property and why they have developed their specific forms and policies. Archives should engage their critics in debate, representing the rights and concerns of the communities and individuals whose collections they hold. Archives and other institutions should make their opinions and expert knowledge available when new regulations are being created covering materials customarily held in archives.

5. Collectors should review their collections carefully for material that is confidential or secret or reveals culturally restricted information. If such materials are found, collectors should contact the artists, performers, or speakers and ask for written authorization to use the materials; deposit them in archives; and make them available for nonprofit educational use of all kinds in the future. When preparing materials for deposit in an archive, collectors should inform the archivists in writing of any sensitive materials for which written agreements have not already been obtained, including suggestions on how to handle the materials.

6. Collectors should review new contracts with the archives or other receiving institutions very carefully to be sure they accord with

the implicit or explicit agreements through which the materials were collected; learn about how to obtain rights to materials collected in the field and assist community members with rights issues before returning to the field; and instruct students and interns in the significance of contracts and the importance of collecting rights as well as recordings during their research.

7. Universities should train researchers in appropriate methodology for recording and receiving rights to use cultural materials. Such training should be part of all research methods classes and should be available to scholars of all ages. All researchers should go to the field with rights information forms in English and the local language and with video cameras; they should have enough training to be able to explain the forms to the people they work with. All students should be exposed to the issues of intellectual property before they start research of any kind to avoid perpetuating a tradition of poor documentation and permissions.

I started this paper with the image of a confused and frustrated horse simultaneously kicked and reined in. When a horse is kicked and the reins give it a direction to go, it will take off. I hope that archives and collectors, frustrated by the lack of direction so far, will move quickly and decisively and become proactive in the area of intellectual property, always keeping in mind the ethical obligations of their materials and their long-term importance to the communities whose traditions they preserve.

Recommended Reading

There is a huge body of literature on intellectual property, ranging from how to get your song published to detailed discussions of a variety of national and international agreements. An outstanding resource for information related to traditional music is the Web site created by Anthony McCann, "Links In Some Way Relevant to my Thesis on Copyright and Traditional Music" **www.ul.ie/~iwmc/research/anthonymccann/thesis_links.html**.

An informative and enjoyable book on the general issues of intellectual property today is *Shamans, Software, and Spleens* (Boyle 1996). The *UNESCO Copyright Bulletin* has several articles on the intellectual property law and indigenous peoples and is representative of the issues being raised in that body (Massey and Stephens 1998). A lively debate on the subject by a group of anthropologists can be found in the article by Michael Brown (1998).

The literature within audiovisual archiving is considerably smaller. It includes a series of articles in the publications of the Association of Recorded Sound Collections, articles in the publications of the International Association of Sound and Audiovisual Archives, and others (Jabbour 1983; Mills 1996; Seeger 1992, 1996).

REFERENCES

Ammann, Raymond. 2000. The Archive Works of the Vanuatu Cultural Centre to Preserve and Maintain Melanesian Music. Paper presented at the conference "100 Years of the Berlin Phonogramm-Archiv" in Berlin, October 2000.

Boyle, James. 1996. *Shamans, Software, and Spleens.* Cambridge: Harvard University Press.

Brown, Michael F. 1998. Can Culture be Copyrighted? *Current Anthropology* 19(2):193-222.

Jabbour, Alan. 1983. Folklore Protection and National Patrimony: Developments and Dilemmas in the Legal Protection of Folklore. *Copyright Bulletin* 17(1):10-14.

Massey, Rachel, and Christopher Stephens. 1998. Intellectual Property Rights, the Law and Indigenous People's Art. *UNESCO Copyright Bulletin* 32(4).

Mills, Sherylle. 1996. Indigenous Music and the Law: An Analysis of National and International Legislation. *Yearbook for Traditional Music* 28:57-86.

Seeger, Anthony. 1992. Ethnomusicology and Music Law. *Ethnomusicology* 36(3):345-60.

______. 1996. Ethnomusicologists, Archives, Professional Organizations, and the Shifting Ethics of Intellectual Property. *Yearbook for Traditional Music* 28:87–105.

Marx, Karl. 1972 [1851]. The Eighteenth Brummaire of Louis Bonapart. In *The Marx-Engels Reader*, edited by Robert C. Tucker. New York: W. W. Norton.

RIGHTS MANAGEMENT:
Summary, Responses, and Discussion

Summary

Anthony Seeger began his summary of rights management issues by linking the issue of intellectual property with preservation. The best way to keep folklore alive, he reminded the audience, is through other people. Folklore is a lived experience and art form; it is not to be fossilized and preserved. Making it possible for people to use, reuse, and recreate folk heritage is vital to its survival. Rights management, therefore, is at the very heart of both preservation and access. Folklore by its nature is a web of rights, obligations, and mutual significances.

We need to answer the question of whom the archives are for, which is another way of asking who owns culture. At a time when privacy concerns are growing in the United States, largely because of the expanded access and distribution available through the Web, none are touched more deeply by privacy issues than the folklorist and those whose culture has been recorded by folklorists. Folklorists do not own the content of their documentation and they must actively involve the creators or those recorded in securing rights for dissemination.

Speaking from his experience as the former director of a folklore archives, Mr. Seeger urged that institutions in custody of traditional materials periodically conduct a systematic review of how they manage their access and use rights. This means that old agreements that are outdated—too restricted or do not address new media rights—must be renegotiated.

Responses

> John Simson, Recording Industry of America
> Rayna Green, Smithsonian Institution

John Simson began his remarks with advice about clearing rights with major recording labels. While recognizing that the participants may have had bad experiences of their own with companies, he said that adopting an adversarial relationship is usually counterproductive. Users have an obligation to know what their own rights and limitations are as well as those of the companies and rights holders. Nothing substitutes for knowledge of the Copyright Act, especially Sections 107 and 108. Knowledge of case law is equally important for understanding fair use and how it works, because most fair use exemptions are decided case by case. He warned that certain contracts between a donor and an institution can be far more restrictive than copyright would ever be. It is important to negotiate contracts that respect the rights of the donor and of those documented but also provide for access in some form.

Rayna Green set the stage for her remarks by saying that the issues before us are not about the size of our bandwidth but the depth of our souls. These issues are fundamentally ethical, and even technological means should work to implement ethical solutions. Intellectual property issues are about who owns history, who can control it, and who benefits from it or gets harmed by it. In traditional communities not everyone has the right to knowledge; this fact alone puts traditional and Western societies into conflict when coming to terms with rights to access, use, and reuse. She referred to most of the documentation currently in libraries, museums, and archives being there as the result of robbery but said that a way to deal honorably with this legacy is to work with descendants of the communities documented to determine how best to deal with present-day access to this knowledge. Start with simple questions: Do you want this knowledge or song or performance to be recorded? Do you want it to be preserved by yourself, by a third party, or not at all? What are your interests in this documentation and what are your needs for access or control? It is incumbent on folklorists, ethnomusicologists, and anthropologists to ask these questions in the context of the community from which the knowledge emerges. Sit and talk with people in their own communities and discuss not only how their community would define and document itself but also what their ethical understanding is of how to treat this documentation over time. Best of all is to train members of the community to document and preserve.

Discussion

These three speakers, touching on law, ethics, and professional practices, sparked an exploration of the very fundamentals of the business of those who document communities and their creativity.

Ethics

Some participants argued that there seemed to be a gulf between the ethical and the legal—what people should do and what the law allows them to do. Mr. Simson urged participants to press their legal counsel to explain to them not only what is legally sanctioned but also what is ethical and what course of action or lack of action would lead to the greatest good for all parties concerned. Law originated as an attempt to codify ethical behavior and to generalize it objectively. No one should use law to hide from an ethical responsibility.

The American Folklore Society adopted a code of ethics in 1987 that asserts the primary responsibility in research is owed to those studied. Their dignity and privacy must be honored. When knowledge is shared and information gathered on the basis of trust between persons, those who agreed to be studied must be safeguarded from a breach of trust.

Several participants challenged both Mr. Seeger's and Ms. Green's invocation of the community as some ethical core. Who defines the community? Is it not true that many traditional cultures are in fact patriarchal and oppressive and withhold information from women and minors for the purpose of subjugating them? How are researchers entering a community for a documentation project to know which voices to listen to, which voices constitute the community?

Others asked about the ethics of the library and archival communities. What about their professional commitment to equal access to information? Although some contemporary Western voices say that information wants to be free, Ms. Green would answer that knowledge is always property and those who create it have the right to take it to the grave with them. In her view, people from traditions in which knowledge belongs to a community object to making information and knowledge into commodities. Moreover, they do not believe that knowledge per se belongs in the public domain. The inherent conflicts that are aroused on this subject were acknowledged, and it seemed clear that frank and respectful communication was the first step to finding mutually acceptable resolutions. Given the importance of this work, consensus emerged that a large group including all stakeholders and experts, from lawyers and folklorists to ethicists and community members, should convene to establish ethical guidelines that could be adopted by professional associations, taught in schools, made available online, and so forth.

The Law

The law is an area of ambiguity and conflict even though it is created to be an instrument for regulation and conciliation. Law attempts to codify ethical practice but, like ethics, is bound by culture and subject to being interpreted differently by those with different interests. Copyright law was designed to protect neither traditional ideas nor original ideas but rather the original expression of an idea, which leaves many traditional arts and artists unprotected. How the law will play out in the digital realm is not at all clear. One lawyer pointed out that putting archival, unpublished materials on the Web, for example, for the simple sake of increasing access may be a form of publishing and may change the rights status of that work. In the many cases in which we simply cannot establish rights, we should find a way to free these materials from potential silent death that results if they are never made available. Rights in the digital realm are highly ambiguous, which has led many archives to be overcautious and restrict access for largely defensive reasons. The increasingly proprietary or aggressive practices of distributors and producers have infected the legal cultures in archives, universities, and public institutions in general, making them more cautious in protecting fair use.

Property laws differ from one country to another even though the Berne Convention and World Intellectual Property Organization have attempted to harmonize national distinctions in the context of a global marketplace. Many participants were also concerned about moral rights, a rather fuzzy concept in the United States. When a record company holds materials from release for defensive purposes, for example, because they simply have no good records about rights inherent in certain materials, what recourse do we have? A European colleague contended that the extension of rights forward and backward in time in Europe is really hampering the essential work of libraries and archives and cautioned that too much protection will result in massive losses of heritage materials.

Education and Training

All agreed that it is imperative that legal and ethical issues be incorporated into formal education programs for scholars who tend to think of themselves as interested in content alone. They must be educated about the law, sensitive to the concerns of the communities with which they are working, and conscientious about seeking permissions from those whom they are documenting. They must also find out whether the people whom they record have the right to perform the works in question. Training for midcareer professionals should be offered regularly by scholarly societies, and focus sessions on rights management should be a regular part of annual meetings. Web-based training or information sites for those outside professional communities should be instituted to begin the critical transfer of skills to members of the communities. Institutions should codify all the information they have about the rights in the materials they hold and let researchers know on entry to the archives that this information is available to be consulted. There is also an urgent need to capture complex rights information in metadata for materials made available digitally.

Advocacy

Many participants expressed frustration that they had so little voice in the recent legislative activity surrounding digital copyright, but lawyers present insisted that advocacy is possible without having the financial resources available to entertainment companies. Advocacy should be seen as part of the ethical responsibility of those who understand the value of folk heritage. Education of lawmakers through their constituents, for example, can be a powerful way of alerting legislators to what is at stake.

Above all, discussions of rights—be they the rights of those documented to control access to information about them or of researchers to have access to music held in record company vaults because of lack of proper clearance information—must be grounded in a firm understanding that rights imply relationships. Stakeholders should develop what some participants called a map of the law that charts these relationships.

Concluding Discussion and Recommendations

The salient innovation of the symposium was the gathering of many experts who have few or no opportunities to talk and develop collaborations. Despite the diversity of experience and interest, consensus emerged about the nature of the problem—extending far beyond preservation—and the solutions—extending far beyond technological fixes bought with additional funding. It was clear that each sector that was represented, from archives to the law, holds part of the solution, and only collaboration will achieve lasting progress. The way to engender collaboration and achieve scalable results depends urgently on continuing the dialogues that began at the meeting.

The diversity of the group attending the symposium was itself a common topic, and most discussions revealed a general lack of coordination in need of immediate remedy. Suggestions for organized coordination included the formation of interdisciplinary committees that could pool resources and information and develop standards, and the formation of advocacy groups to create new partnerships, raise funds, and generate public interest. Enlisting the new executive director of the American Folklore Society as a general coordinator was also proposed.

Each group that developed strategies for improved access, preservation, and rights management agreed on the need to

- develop a Web portal to provide links to resources and reference materials and to facilitate the coordination of the efforts of diverse communities;
- increase public awareness about heritage collections and the crisis they face;
- develop best practices guidelines and standards;
- develop better education and training opportunities for researchers, archivists, audio engineers, and community members;

- develop partnerships among the technology, corporate, and entertainment sectors;
- extend the reach of expertise and resources to regional and local levels in ways that include but also go beyond the Web portal;
- create and fund teams of experts who could work as consultants, traveling to different sites to lead workshops, provide expertise, provide services, etc.; and
- establish regional centers for preservation and distributed access when appropriate.

Specific recommendations for the three areas follow, along with the names of the organizations best positioned to play leading roles.

Access

1. *Develop an interdisciplinary online portal*
   Develop an interdisciplinary online portal that will provide access to existing materials and resources for sound archives. [Society of Ethnomusicology in collaboration with Harvard University]

2. *Create the ethnographic thesaurus*
   Convene the Ethnographic Thesaurus Working Group to develop a proposal for submission to the National Endowment for the Humanities for the July 2001 deadline. The proposal will provide planning grant funds to shape this project with a clear scope of work, budget, and an institutional home. [American Folklife Center, American Folklore Society, May 2001]

3. *Develop metadata schemes*
   Investigate and develop the use of Dublin Core or other relevant metadata schemes to facilitate the creation and sharing of descriptions and indexes of unpublished ethnographic recordings. [University of Washington, Harvard University, Library of Congress, Michigan State University, American Folklore Society, Society of Ethnomusicologists, and others]

4. *Develop regional facilities for local access*
   Explore the designation of regional facilities that might provide data migration and other resources to small and mid-sized archives. [Library of Congress; Indiana University; Harvard University; University of California, Los Angeles; others]

5. *Disseminate information about the symposium results*
   All participants include a link to the symposium Web site and sound preservation information. [All]

Preservation

1. *Develop an urgency matrix*
   Develop and post on the symposium Web site an urgency matrix and best practices preservation guidelines for small to mid-sized

archives. This document will not be comprehensive but should include recommendations for affordable and reasonable preservation of the most common recording media (reel-to-reel tape, audio cassettes, video cassettes, digital audiotape, etc.) with cost models for treatment and equipment recommendations. [Association for Recorded Sound Collections, Audio Engineering Society]

2. *Develop a magnetic media manual*
   Ensure that the Research Libraries Group magnetic media manual is translated into simple language to be useful for folklorists, ethnomusicologists, collectors, and others with sound collections. Have a link from Research Libraries Group site to the symposium Web site. [Research Libraries Group]

3. *Develop guidelines and best practices for capture*
   Develop and publish a set of guidelines and best practices for information capture, metadata, etc. to cover all sound media by 2002. [Audio Engineering Society, Library of Congress, Association for Recorded Sound Collections]

4. *Publicize standards developed for audiovisual facilities*
   Publicize standards developed by the Library of Congress for its Culpeper Facility to be a model for handling cultural legacy audio and visual materials and update national standards as needed. [Library of Congress]

5. *Develop scalable models for digital preservation*
   Provide expert service and production facilities to small and mid-sized archives for digital preservation and data migration. [Library of Congress, Digital Library Federation]

6. *Develop a registry of vendors*
   Develop a list of reputable vendors of equipment and services for sound preservation, especially firms able to handle legacy formats. [Library of Congress, Association for Recorded Sound Collections]

7. *Recruit and train technicians*
   Encourage technical and engineering schools to train the next generation of expert technicians for audio preservation and include legacy format competency. [Audio Engineering Society, Library of Congress, Association for Recorded Sound Collections]

8. *Disseminate collections survey results*
   Disseminate collections survey results from the symposium and provide this information to other surveys, such as the National Recording Preservation Board at the Library of Congress, to ensure that small and mid-sized archives are included in national statistics. [Council on Library and Information Resources, American Folklife Center]

9. *Develop a registry of recordings*
   Track the existence and location of preserved audio recordings with machine-readable records and online registries to guard against duplication of effort and maximize preservation of unique recordings.

10. *Develop training workshops*
    Develop a series of workshops where national and large university archives can provide training and guidance to small and mid-sized archives on sound preservation. This could be a "SWAT team" approach, with several experts who might be called on as needed, perhaps to approach the National Endowment for the Humanities for funding through the Preservation Assistance Grants category. [Association of Recorded Sound Collections in collaboration with American Folklife Center; Library of Congress; Harvard University; Indiana University; University of California, Los Angeles; others]

Intellectual Property Rights

1. *Establish a listserv*
   Establish a listserv to continue the conversations of the symposium. [American Folklife Center, American Folklore Society, January 2001]

2. *Develop ethical guidelines for dissemination*
   Convene a larger group to discuss and develop ethical guidelines for publication and online presentation of audio recordings from ethnographic archives. Include ethicists, artists, and community members. The group should consider the application of intellectual property and copyright law as it applies to ethnographic field recordings. The group should also map relationships for materials already collected and investigate the standards used by local communities, tribal groups, and artists for the issues surrounding intellectual property rights. [National Endowment for the Humanities, Library of Congress, Recording Industry Association of America, ASCAP, BMI]

3. *Develop model contracts*
   Develop model agreements and issue lists for institutions to access and consult on the issue of intellectual property rights vis-à-vis the collector, the artist or tradition bearer, and the archive or institution. These model agreements could be posted online through the Federal Communications Commission symposium Web site. [Library of Congress; Smithsonian Institution; Indiana University; Harvard University; University of California, Los Angeles]

4. *Renegotiate existing contracts if they are inadequate*
   Encourage archivists and collectors to renegotiate inadequate contracts and agreements for clear rights protection. [All]

5. *Create a database of public domain materials*
   Create and maintain a database of materials in the public domain and digitize these materials on a priority basis. [All]

6. *Establish a liaison to industry*
   Establish a liaison to the commercial music industry to facilitate access to back catalogs and out-of-print recordings held in commercial vaults. [National Academy of Recording Arts and Sciences, Recording Industry Association of America, institutional repositories]

7. *Provide rights training*
   Provide archival employees with ongoing training on rights issues. [All]

8. *Publish a guide to rights*
   Develop an online and print publication on the basic intellectual property rights issues and use of archival collections, and disseminate this publication to sound archives. Perhaps model this on the publication *Working with Folk Materials in New York State*. [New York Folklore Society, American Folklore Society, Society of Ethnomusicology]

9. *Update existing fieldwork handbooks*
   Update existing fieldwork handbooks to include training and guidelines on rights and issues of privacy along with advice on not depositing materials that may be too problematical. [All]

10. *Offer continuing education*
    Offer continuing education at professional meetings on intellectual property rights, privacy in metadata, and other issues. [American Folklore Society, Society of Ethnomusicology, Association for Recorded Sound Collections, American Library Association]

11. *Represent copyright interests to lawmakers*
    Form a committee to address copyright law. Explore increasing access to out-of-print recordings through compulsory licensing. [Library of Congress, Recording Industry Association of America, BMI, Music Library Association, American Library Association, American Folklore Society, Association for Recorded Sound Collections]

12. *Update interlibrary loan regulations*
    Update interlibrary loan regulations in the copyright law, work toward compulsory licensing of music that companies withhold because of uncertain rights, and encourage Congress to conduct oversight hearings addressing fair use issues. [All]

APPENDIX I
Conference Participants

Larry Applebaum
Library of Congress

John Perry Barlow
Electronic Frontier Foundation

Phyllis Barney
North American Folk Music & Dance Alliance

Robert Baron
National Endowment for the Humanities

Christina Barr
Vermont Folklife Center

Jane Beck
Vermont Folklife Center

Barry Bergey
National Endowment for the Arts

Deborah Boykin
Mississippi Band of Choctaw Indian Tribal Archives

Richard Bradshaw
IBM

Erika Brady
Western Kentucky University

Samuel Brylawski
Library of Congress

Peggy Bulger
American Folklife Center

Andrea Camp
Institute for Civil Society

Emory Campbell
Penn Center

Candie Carawan
Highlander Research and Education Center

Guy Carawan
Highlander Research and Education Center

Anna Chairetakis
Association for Cultural Equity

Elizabeth Cohen
Cohen Acoustical Inc.

Dudley Connell
National Council for Traditional Arts

Jennifer Cutting
American Folklife Center

Robin Dale
Research Libraries Group

Virginia Danielson
Harvard University

Robert Aubry Davis
RADMAN Productions

Tom Diamant
Arhoolie Records

Elaine Eff
Maryland Historical Trust

George Farr
National Endowment for the Humanities

Shelley Feist
The Pew Charitable Trusts

Kelly Feltault
Cultural Crossings

William Ferris
National Endowment for the Humanities

Jeff Field
National Endowment for the Humanities

Suzanne Flandreau
Columbia College

Carl Fleischhauer
Library of Congress

LeeEllen Friedland
Library of Congress

Daryl Friedman
The Recording Academy

Janet Gertz
Columbia University

Gerald Gibson
Library of Congress

Judith Gray
American Folklife Center

Rayna Green
Smithsonian Institution

Steve Green
Western Folklife Center

Elana Hadler
Duke University

Martha Hanson
Syracuse University

Mickey Hart
360 Degrees Productions

Joe Hickerson
Independent Scholar

Ann Hoog
American Folklife Center

John Howell
Library of Congress

Tanya Irvine
University of North Carolina

Alan Jabbour
Independent Scholar

E. Scott Johnson, Esq.
Ober, Kaler, Grimes and Shriver

Jeanne Harrah Johnson
Nevada Arts Council Archives

Cathy Hiebert Kerst
American Folklife Center

John Knowles
Country Music Foundation

Charles Kolb
National Endowment for the Humanities

Edward Komara
Blues Archives

Richard Kurin
Smithsonian Institution

Geraldine Laudati
University of Wisconsin-Madison

Melissa Levine
Library of Congress

Suzanne M. Lodato
Andrew W. Mellon Foundation

Jack Loeffler
Museum of New Mexico

Kip Lornell
George Washington University

Ellen Lovell
White House

Marsha Maguire
University of Washington

Allan McConnell
Library of Congress

Susan McCormick
Talking History: Journal of MultiMedia

Brad McCoy
Library of Congress

Cheryl Mollicone
GRAMMY Foundation

Jeffrey Norman
Grateful Dead Productions

Bill Nowlin
Rounder Records

Elizabeth Higgins Null
Independent Scholar

Elena M. Paul, Esq.
Washington Area Lawyer for the Arts

Betsy Peterson
Fund for Folk Culture

Mimi Pickering
Appalshop Inc.

Jeff Place
Smithsonian Institution

Frank Proschan
Smithsonian Institution

Jo Radner
American Folklore Society

Carl Rahkonen
Indiana University of Pennsylvania

Sayuri Rajapakse
Library of Congress

Tom Rankin
Duke University

Dean Rehberger
MATRIX

Mark Roosa
Library of Congress

David Sanjek
BMI Archives

Henry Sapoznik
Living Traditions

Barbara Sawka
Stanford University

Dietrich Schueller
Akademie der Wissenschaften Phonogrammarchiv

Michael Seadle
Michigan State University

Anthony Seeger
University of California, Los Angeles

Michael Shapiro, Esq.
International Intellectual Property Institute

Dan Sheehy
Smithsonian Folkways Recordings

Art Silverman
National Public Radio

Christine Sims
Acoma Language Retention Project

John Simson
Soundexchange

Abby Smith
Council on Library and Information Resources

Moira Smith
Indiana University

Stephanie Smith
Smithsonian Institution

Steve Smolian
Smolian Sound Studios

Atesh Sonneborn
Smithsonian Institution

Louise Spear
University of California, Los Angeles

Chris Strachwitz
Arhoolie Records

Susan Sturtevant
Museum of New Mexico

John Suter
New York Heritage Documentation Project

Michael Taft
American Folklife Center

Karen Taussig-Lux
New York Folklore Society

Janet Topp-Fargion
British Library

Mike Turpin
Library of Congress

Steve Weiss
Southern Folklife Collection

Randy Williams
Utah State University

Joe Wilson
National Council for the Traditional Arts

Nora Yeh
American Folklife Center

Peggy Yocom
George Mason University

Gerry Zahavi
University of Albany-SUNY

APPENDIX II
Survey of Folk Heritage Collections:
Summary of Results

In the second half of 2000, the American Folklife Center, in partnership with the American Folklore Society and the Society for Ethnomusicology, conducted a nationwide survey of unpublished recorded ethnographic audio collections. The purpose was to determine whether the vast amount of folk heritage materials gathered by professionals over a half century is entering safely into the cultural heritage of the nation. Anecdotes are legion about the plight of personal academic collections that receive little or no protection from environmental damage, publicly funded documentation projects that are inaccessible to the public and at risk of decay, and significant collections in repositories that cannot be accessed because of the ambiguity or lack of records of release for access. How can we develop a national plan for securing preservation and extending access to folk heritage collections when we lack essential data about their state?

As a way to begin gathering information, we focused on unpublished materials and surveyed organizations and individuals most likely to hold important collections of them. The survey was sent to the members of American Folklore Society and Society for Ethnomusicology and to other known collectors not belonging to these societies. We surveyed both large and small repositories and agencies conducting documentation projects, such as state folklore offices and museums. These are referred to as organizational collections. We also surveyed private collections held by individuals who have not deposited their recordings into a publicly accessible repository. These are referred to as individual collections. We mailed 2,000 surveys and received 297 responses—from 178 organizations and 119 individuals.

The survey began with questions designed to profile the collection and the infrastructure supporting it. The remainder of the questions addressed preservation, access, and intellectual property rights, with about 10 questions on each topic.

This summary of the survey results distills the salient facts uncovered and points to major gaps in our knowledge and understanding of what folklore and ethnomusicology has been recorded, where those collections can be found, how accessible they are, and whether present and future researchers are entitled to gain access to them for research purposes. It was the expectation of those who designed the survey that it would result in a baseline data set about the nation's recorded folklore, something sorely needed by archivists, librarians, researchers, and communities that have been documented. Although the results are profoundly interesting and paint of vivid picture of the state of collections, not enough data were gathered to serve that purpose. Rather, this survey reveals where the state of knowledge ends and ignorance begins.

Clear trends emerge from these data, the most important being the functional and intellectual disconnect between those responsible for creating the collections and those charged with caring for them. A simple example of this can be seen in the data showing that folklorists receive grant funds for project documentation but not for creating access systems or planning for preservation. In other words, the creators of folk heritage documentation do not plan for the life cycle of their evidence. Another example is the small number of people and organizations who hold collections and have any funds allocated for their care and use. The list goes on.

Collection Profiles

Funding

Individual collectors operate overwhelmingly without a budget—that is, specially allocated funds that come from a known source—although a small percentage (9 percent) of respondents indicated that they use their personal funds to support the maintenance of their collections. More individuals (12 percent) indicated that they receive funding to conduct documentation but not to manage the collection or prepare it for deposit after documentation. Organizational collections fell mostly within two categories of budget support—those operating on less than $10,000 annually (36 percent) and those operating without any allocations at all (37 percent). In other words, most organizations receive funding only slightly better than do the individual collections located in private homes.

Professional Background

Most organizations (68 percent) have a full-time staff. Fifty-three percent of the responding organizations have staff members with a professional background in folklore. Sixty-one percent reported having staff members with a professional background in archives and collections management or library science. Among individual collectors, the findings were quite different: only 10 percent of the individuals responding reported having any training in archives, collection management, or library science. As the budget figures imply, these individuals may know about creating documentation but not about the need to care for that documentation.

Age of Collections

The age of these collections and the media on which they are recorded have implications for their preservation and access. Only 13 percent of all collections contain materials recorded before 1940; nearly all are organizational collections. Of these, the pre-1940 recordings make up 25 percent of their collections. Further analysis shows that most of the items in state folklore collections and individual collections were recorded between 1981 and the present.

Formats of Collections

Over 90 percent of all collections have cassette tapes, and these cassettes constitute the largest category of format, an average of over 90 percent of both individual and organizational collections. Older formats such as lacquer discs, wire, wax cylinders, and aluminum discs are found only in organizational collections.

Preservation

Storage Conditions

Analog audiovisual collections in all formats are very vulnerable to physical degradation, and natural processes such as the separation of signal from substrate can be either significantly accelerated or retarded by environmental conditions. Only 49 percent of organizational collections are kept under climate-controlled conditions in which the heat and humidity levels are monitored and controlled for stability. In looking at responses to questions about storage conditions, it became clear that most individuals either did not make any attempt to stabilize their collections or mistakenly thought that domestic heating, ventilating, and air conditioning systems constitute climate control. Just over half of the individual respondents (51 percent) kept their recordings in cardboard boxes, either on open shelves or in filing cabinets.

Copies for Access

It was abundantly clear from responses that only large organizations are able to make listening, or reference, copies from preservation masters. Only 12 percent of organizations that operate with budgets of less than $10,000 reported making preservation master copies in at least some cases; most of the state arts agencies and nonprofit organizations do not make a preservation master. Even more distressing, but certainly not surprising, is that most individuals are not even aware of the need to make such masters. They were confused by the questions that distinguished between preservation and reference copies and the original.

Preservation Surveys

Only 18 percent of organizations and 2 percent of individuals have assessed the state of preservation of their collections.

Access

Deposit

Most individuals (79 percent) reported intending to deposit their materials with an organization at some point. Those who were not planning to do so indicated that the documentation either did not have release forms (50 percent) or that the items had poor recording quality, were too sensitive in content, and so forth.

Database Access

Thirty-eight percent of organizations and 80 percent of individuals manage their collections without the use of a database. Although larger organizations use a database to manage their collections, 44 percent of university archives and 50 percent of state and nonprofit agencies cannot retrieve any part of their holdings from their databases.

Public Access

Organizations primarily use indexes and logs as finding aids; although 62 percent of organizations have databases, they do not use them for public access purposes. Moreover, most organizations (68 percent) that use subject headings have devised them themselves, using no common standard. Twenty-three percent use Library of Congress subject headings. Despite present practice, 63 percent of responding organizations said that they favor the creation of standardized subject headings.

The survey sought to identify the biggest users of various collections, but the responses indicate that most organizations show little or no use. Some organizations simply do not anticipate use by the public. Historical societies, museums, nonprofit organizations, and state arts agencies reported very little use of their collections by the public, including academic researchers.

Internet Access

The debates over placing ethnographic and oral history materials on the Web continue, but our survey shows that 90 percent of all respondents do not have any of their collections available through the Web.[1] Of the 133 respondents who reported having none of their collections on the Web, 92 did not answer the question about influences on the decision to make collections accessible on the Internet. Of those who did respond, restrictions, privacy issues, and funding were the major factors hindering Web-based public access. Not surprisingly, only institutions with full-time staff members reported having some collections online.

Intellectual Property Rights

Release Forms

Only 25 percent of organizations reported having release forms for the greater bulk (76–100 percent) of their collections. An alarming 39 percent of all individuals do not have release forms for their materi-

---

[1] This can be attributed to many factors, including lack of funding, personnel, technology, and computerized finding aids such as databases. Many collections also reported that they did not have Web sites.

als; most of them hold materials recorded between 1961 and 1980, and 40 percent of these collectors are ethnomusicologists.

This section of the survey contained much handwritten commentary from respondents. The most interesting commentaries were from university professors and archivists stating that students did not need to obtain release forms, archivists and fieldworkers claiming that the other party was responsible for procuring release forms, and fieldworkers conducting research in developing countries stating that releases were not necessary in those parts of the world.

Responsibility for Releases

When asked about who is responsible for obtaining permission to document, organizations responded that either the project coordinator (37 percent), the fieldworker (25 percent), or—most baffling—the archivist (21 percent) was. Only 40 percent of individuals declared that it was their responsibility as fieldworker to obtain releases.

Income

When asked how they generate income from their collections, 72 percent of respondents claim not to generate income or cost recovery from their collections through royalties, copyrights, or duplication and processing fees. Nonprofit agencies make up the majority of organizations generating income from development of products from their collections. Only two state arts agencies reported using their collections in this manner.